D1077652

For Joyce, who turns all the work
of marriage into play.

GOD
THE SHORT VERSION

Peter Lundstrom

LION

A Lion Book
an imprint of
Lion Hudson plc
Wilkinson House, Jordan Hill Road,
Oxford OX2 8DR, England
www.lionhudson.com

UK ISBN 978 0 7459 5312 0
US ISBN 978 0 8254 6272 6

First edition 2008
10 9 8 7 6 5 4 3 2 1 0

Acknowledgments
Scripture quotations taken from the *Holy Bible, New International Version*, copyright © 1973, 1978, 1984 International Bible Society. Used by permission of Zondervan and Hodder & Stoughton Limited. All rights reserved. The 'NIV' and 'New International Version' trademarks are registered in the United States Patent and Trademark Office by International Bible Society. Use of either trademark requires the permission of International Bible Society. UK trademark number 1448790.

The text paper used in this book has been made from wood independently certified as having come from sustainable forests.

A catalogue record for this book is available
from the British Library

Typeset in 9/12 ITC Stone Serif
Printed and bound in Malta

Distributed by:
UK: Marston Book Services Ltd, PO Box 269, Abingdon,
Oxon OX14 4YN
USA: Trafalgar Square Publishing, 814 N Franklin Street,
Chicago, IL 60610
USA Christian Market: Kregel Publications, PO Box 2607,
Grand Rapids, MI 49501

Contents

CHAPTER 1

A Quick Chat About the Inexpressible

Except for the Buddha, each of us desires something. At birth, we want food, sleep and dry diapers. In youth, we reach for love and success. Years pass and our desires wax, wane and change. But most of us, whether early or late in life, find within our hearts the deepest of all desires. We want freedom from confusion and futility. We want liberation from suffering and death. We want limitless love and infinite grace. We want what is beyond ourselves: we want to embrace and be embraced by the fullness of life.

In short, we want God.

But usually in small doses. We have all heard that name before and simply saying it raises a reflexive babble. Our fears, questions, assumptions, presumptions and misperceptions make it hard to talk about God.

So how do we start? In this chapter, we will begin with ourselves and some of our basic questions. In the short chapters to come, by looking at the world's major religions, we will see how people around the globe understand God and how they agree and disagree about 'him', 'her' and 'them'. In the final chapter, we will consider some basic temptations that confront any person who searches for God.

Full Disclosure

There is no such thing as a neutral author – or reader – since each of us can only speak and listen out of our own understanding. In this book, you will certainly find, especially in later chapters, an underlying Christian perspective and more time spent examining Judeo-Christian scriptures. But you will also see humankind's great religions and world views, Christianity included, clearly enough to understand their basic ideas and compare them for yourself. All in all, you will enjoy a satisfying serving of fresh, wholesome food for thought.

Now for the basic questions.

What Do We Want to Know?

We want a simple, sturdy, engaging introduction to who or what God may be. But since it is God we are discussing, be prepared for the unexpected. Furthermore, it is a good bet that any tour in the vicinity of the Divine will not always be comfy, a proposition confirmed in most of the world's scriptures, which say starkly that no one can behold God and live. Fortunately, our intentions are more humble. Even so, we will soon be out of our league, asking questions whose answer will overshadow us utterly.

A Larger View of Things

For starters, let us expand our thinking with a few quick observations about a much smaller, simpler subject – the universe.

The story begins billions of years ago.

But how much is a billion (1,000,000,000) – not in the abstract but on a human scale? To get a clearer idea, try this. Make a literal career of counting to a billion by working at it eight hours a day, five days a week, and let each second of your working week represent a year. Start counting the seconds on Monday morning and, at the end of the day on Friday, you will have counted 144,000 seconds, representing 144,000 years. An excellent start, but be patient. At this rate, you will not count your first billion years until you have worked for 134 of your own actual years.

But, eventually, you get there. Congratulations. Now repeat the process nineteen more times. Sorry, no breaks.

At the end of your 2,680th year on the job, you will reach 20 billion. At last, looking back on the long millennia of your counting career, you will better appreciate the fact that our universe is about 20 billion years old.

And because the universe's elements were forged early, you also, in a sense, are 20 billion years old. Not only is your matter exceedingly old, it is also inconceivably strange. If you search for its smallest building blocks, you will encounter a paradox – the closer you look, the less solid stuff you find. At the foundations of everything, atoms are virtually devoid of solid matter.

You would see this immediately if you could expand a single atom for study. Enlarge it from its everyday size (100 million make a row about a centimetre long) to, say, the size of the earth. Alas, that is not large enough, since an earth-sized atom would still be much too small for study with the naked eye. In fact, you must expand the atom far more, until its diameter matches the distance from the earth to the moon.

At this scale, comparing this atom to the earth is like comparing a basketball to a pea. But your interplanetary atomic basketball has no surface – only a vast and hazy outer shell. Within it, the atom's few electrons sweep indeterminately through a 400,000-kilometre-wide virtual void, since the only matter in this stupendous nothingness lies at its centre, where some protons and neutrons form the atom's nucleus, an almost imperceptible cluster about 380 metres wide – less than the length of four soccer pitches. And even though the nucleus contains most of the atom's mass, it too remains largely empty, because each of its few protons and neutrons is about a tenth as wide as the nucleus. In turn, each proton and neutron consists of three quarks. They also exist in vast isolation, since each quark is the size of a golf ball. Beyond the quark are even greater emptiness and more uncharted mystery.

All of which simply means that you, like everything in existence, are made almost entirely of empty space.

Lost in Space

Now transport your barely material self to earth's remotest outback, wait for the darkest night and look up. You can see about 5,000 stars. The closest is Proxima Centauri, a little less than 25 trillion miles away. Have any real idea what a trillion is?

Note that all the stars you see are located within our galaxy, which contains about 200 billion stars in all. Our entire galaxy, in turn, is less than a mote among the estimated total of 125 billion galaxies in the universe.

But even the universe offers no static limit. Ever since its incandescent birth, the universe itself has been expanding at nearly the speed of light. More overwhelming still, theoretical physicists suggest there may be infinite universes. A game of checkers can generate hundreds of billions of possible outcomes. Could there be a universe for each? Why not? A few hundred billion universes would be nothing in the infinite scheme of things.

Feeling smaller? Yet, so far, we have grappled with nothing more than *size*, a category that does not even apply to God.

Who Wants to Know?

If meeting God were like meeting the Queen, who would decline an introduction? Curiosity alone would compel even a Richard Dawkins to venture a quick audience with the Ancient of Days.

But meeting God requires far more than an opening in one's calendar; it requires an open heart. This search begins only when we lay aside arrogance. Especially in our materialist era, we may conceive of the Divine as merely another kind of problem to be solved – which, in turn, may lead us to assume that we are the scientists and God is the stuff on the slide under the microscope.

Of course, no such God could exist except as the creation of our own hubris. This Greek word translates as 'pride', not in our current sense of 'self-respect' but in the older, deeper sense of 'self-righteousness' or 'arrogance'. With wonderful astringency, the 1911 *Catholic Encyclopedia* says that pride is 'the excessive love of one's own excellence'. Hubris persuades a man to secretly adore even his own humility. In time, pride may acclimatize us to the idea that we are well suited to pal around with God – how much different from us can he be? We must rid ourselves, as best we can, from hubris or we will look deep into the well of truth and see only our own reflection.

Fortunately, the antidote to hubris is well known, highly effective, and is the second requirement for our expedition into God. It is humility. Here is a word with a rich family history, descending from an ancient Indo-European root word that means 'earth'. From this same root come our words 'humble', 'human' and 'humus'. As a small exercise in humility, here is the Oxford English Dictionary's description of humus: 'the organic component of soil, formed by the decomposition of leaves and other plant material'. We humans are cousins of humus, which gives us plenty to be humble about.

Now that you know humanity's dirty or, rather, earthy secret, beware the other current, peculiar error of equating 'humility' with 'timidity' or even 'self-loathing'. Humility is the powerful antidote to both hubris and cravenness, since it will not permit us to be either above *or* beneath ourselves or anyone else. Humility is not an exercise in niceness; it is the power by which we see things as they are. In an online essay at www.chabad.org, Jonathan Sacks, the Chief Rabbi of Great Britain, writes that 'true humility is one of the most expansive and life-enhancing of all virtues. It does not mean undervaluing yourself. It means valuing other people… Humility is what opens the world.' So let us shed hubris as best we can, embrace humility and move with fear and trembling beyond ourselves.

This means giving our own presuppositions a close examination, since they always shape the way we ask questions and hear answers. In our search for God, here are three basic questions we must examine for hidden presuppositions.

Is there a God? Well, what do we mean by 'God'? In our era, most of us in the West are so imbued with the concept of monotheism that we instinctively think of a being perfect in virtue and power, without beginning or end. Yet thousands of years ago, in the Ancient Near East, most people thought of God as a being who, though greater than the rest of the created world, was himself a creature, the offspring of Fate or Chaos and subject to them. Do we mean this kind of God? Furthermore, what do we mean by 'is' – does God exist the same way the universe and we do? If so, then perhaps God, like our universe, has a beginning and even, one day, an end. But if God exists differently from matter and is not, therefore, material, then what is he? And where?

What is God? If we ask 'what', then we imply that God is not a person – a very basic and important assumption. If God is without personhood, then how do we, who are persons, relate to it? What if God is impersonal, like the ocean – beautiful, powerful, dangerous, vast? We could not speak of 'him' or 'her' or 'them' but only of 'it'. And while 'it' could of course be admired, could it be worshipped if it is incapable of a personal response? Perhaps this God would be a sort of force, a mystical fire or wind – and might such an impersonal force be available for our control? Or would it be a 'something' that is utterly something else?

Who is God? 'Who' implies that God is a person, so, if we want to ask this question, we must think about persons and relationships. Can a person so beyond our ken be someone that humans can relate to? Would this relationship be anything like the relationships we know among ourselves? Who could qualify to be admitted to this bond?

In short, we humans assume much, as we must if we are to navigate our inner and outer lives. When we ask after the Other, however, we need to examine our assumptions in whole new ways.

Who Wants to Answer?

All the questions we ask about God contain a vital assumption that needs close and sober consideration. The assumption is that God is inclined to reply. But can we presume this of one so infinitely beyond us? After all, if there is a God who is other than some vast material, who is the least bit mighty, then this One is fully capable of remaining inscrutable and is under no obligation to notify us of his existence. In fact, it follows that, unless God cares to reveal himself, it is impossible that we can know or apprehend the slightest true thing about him, let alone him, personally.

But what if a God with personhood exists, is inclined to be known and somehow introduces himself to humans? Then something staggering is unfolding: the Infinite wants to reach us. If we could come to this possibility with no preconceptions, we would see it as something on the scale of contact by an alien galactic civilization, only much, much bigger. Of course the follow-on questions would be all-consuming. If God's self-revealing signal is out there, how do we perceive it for what it is and, additionally, not confuse it with some other bogus 'revelation'? And second, why does God want to be in touch with us? Will this be an ecstatic encounter or an obliterating terror? More than ever, we should proceed humbly, carefully, but also – if God is ringing – with due haste to answer.

Who Wants to Hear?

You may enquire about God and decide there is none. Or your search may bring you face to face with an awesome someone. In either case, you have reached a crossroads. Closing the book on God *or* coming to accept that God exists – could any decision be more momentous? If any decision *could* be greater, what would that imply about the stature of the God you have in mind?

How Do We Begin?

We will go to those with experience. We will consider the understanding of God found in four great categories of belief – pantheism, nontheism, polytheism and monotheism.

Pantheistic religions believe that God consists of the whole of nature. God is within all of nature and nature is God.

Nontheistic belief systems do not search for a God. Buddhism, the world's largest nontheistic system at about 376 million followers,[1] concentrates instead on the cause of human suffering and finds it within every person in the form of 'attachment'. We suffer because we grasp at the illusions of the self and its futile desires. When one sheds every attachment, one sees the world as it is – a unity, with neither 'self' nor 'other'. One has 'awakened' into perfect clarity and is freed forever – not only from suffering, but also from captivity in the unending cycle of birth, death and rebirth. One enters Nirvana, a state beyond every other – even beyond being. Hinduism (900 million followers) claims more adherents than Buddhism, but is not purely nontheistic. This very ancient religion has strong elements of nontheism, but also of pantheism, polytheism and even monotheism. Naturalism (also called atheism) holds that God or gods do not exist and never have, and that the natural world is the only reality. This makes naturalists distinct from the far larger group of agnostics, who claim no certainty one way or the other. The *World Christian Encyclopedia* estimates the number of naturalists worldwide at about 150 million.

Polytheistic religions believe in a vast host of gods who vary widely in character, purpose and influence.

Monotheistic religions believe in a single God, the One who is God alone and unique in every way. The world's three great monotheistic faiths – Christianity (2.1 billion followers), Islam (1.5 billion followers) and their common source, Judaism (14 million followers) – now claim as adherents about 54 per cent of earth's current population.

In the pages ahead, we will look more closely at all these beliefs. For now, take to heart this simple observation from the Bible: 'The fear [reverential awe] of the Lord is the beginning of knowledge' (Proverbs 1:7). The beginning. Who knows where the end will lie?

CHAPTER 2

Atheism: Almighty Reason

For roughly thirty-three centuries, the Western world took the existence of divinity largely for granted. The early millennia of Greek and Roman polytheism were eventually supplanted by succeeding centuries of Christian monotheism, but uninterruptedly and across the entire social order – in the palaces, barracks, farms, academies and the home – first the gods and later God were understood as the central ordering reality who ultimately controlled the vast order of the cosmos and all the affairs of humankind.

However, those theocentric centuries eventually gave way to a new understanding of the world. And this understanding, by comparison, is new indeed. By the eighteenth century, European philosophers had moved mankind to the centre of human affairs, and in the few centuries that followed, the citizenry of Europe had done likewise in everyday life. God moved to the periphery. Today, according to the 2002 Pew Global Attitudes study, a worldwide public opinion survey:

> Secularism is particularly prevalent throughout Europe. Even in heavily Catholic Italy fewer than three-in-ten (27%) people say religion is very important personally, a lack of intensity in belief that is consistent with opinion in other Western European nations.[2]

While the same study showed that more than twice as many people (59 per cent) in the United States said religion is very important in their lives, other polls and surveys support the idea that religion in the United States is on a relative decline.

All of which has made an opening for atheism. This Latin word simply means 'without god(s)' and elegantly defines the atheist conviction. Atheists assert that there is no God or gods. Some prefer other titles, particularly 'naturalism', for several reasons. The first is that the very word 'atheist' leaves them defined by the God in whom they do not believe, which some find burdensome. After all, a Christian or Hindu is unlikely to favour being widely known as an 'infidel', the Muslim term that defines all non-Muslims by the Islam in which they do not believe.

But the second reason is the more substantial, because a word like naturalism points to the basis of this conviction. It holds that nature is the only verifiable reality and that the supernatural realm, being unverifiable, does not exist. Things like galaxies, neutrons, rabbits, cars and humans are made of matter – matter that provides consistent evidence that can be detected and measured. Physical evidence exists for the natural realm, but no such evidence exists for gods, ghosts or miraculous goings-on. Atheists weigh the evidence and conclude that we live in the realm of nature, the only reality there is.

Naturalism

Naturalists have put a solid foundation under these convictions by developing the scientific method. Realized and refined over centuries, the scientific method offers a reliable way to examine the natural world and establish an accurate understanding of it. Only the scientific method yields the hypotheses, the theories and the laws that describe the natural world as it is, not as we suppose it to be.

This way of examining our world and ourselves is vastly powerful, producing endless waves of revolution in the way we understand the workings of our entire cosmos and the ways we use it for our own purposes. It is the scientific method that relocated the sun to the centre of the solar system, deciphered The Big Bang and supplied the electricity for your morning toast and tea.

But naturalism, using the scientific method, has yet to find convincing evidence for the existence of God. Naturalists conclude that a God who leaves no trace of himself in the natural world is only an idea in the mind, not a being who actually exists in the real world. In what way, they might ask, is God different from a child's imaginary friend, a Greek poet's winged horse or a schizophrenic's voices and visitors? God may be in the mind, but he is not in the natural world in which humans dwell.

So, can a modern person, living in an era born of and sustained by the scientific method, find any place for God? Is there still room for him in a scientific cosmos?

At first blush, the answer is no. God cannot be part of a purely scientific world because naturalism excludes God by definition. Naturalism says that it regards as real only those things that can be detected, inspected and measured.

Unreasonably, God Remains
But on closer examination, the answer is yes. Naturalism uses science to look for a God in nature made from the stuff of nature. Yet God, by definition, is inscrutable, beyond our conceiving, above nature and perhaps beyond being as we know it. This puts him well beyond the reach of calipers, microscopes, tevatrons and any other tool of scientific inspection.

But that is the point, says the naturalist. If any God exists, it exists only in the mind. And with the phrase 'only in the mind', another door opens to even deeper and more ancient questions.

The Mind/Body Problem
Since the beginnings of philosophy, the relationship between the mind and the body has been a fundamental mystery. From head to

toe, we are made of matter – fleshy, bony, bloody matter. But in our matter-filled craniums, something else is going on. Accompanying or perhaps emerging from our brains are our thoughts, which are made of – what? And it's not just our thoughts. What is the stuff of love, grief, anger, joy and all our other emotions? Most of all, what is the stuff of our very consciousness, our sense that each of us is a self?

The problem is that our thoughts seem to be made of no stuff at all. The body has arms, legs, a head, a brain and a hefty load of other parts, all of them made of matter. But our thoughts, our sense of self – in short, our minds – are like no other part of the body. They have no matter. Yet they are in and of matter. In fact, our minds are what animate the matter of our bodies. In short, our immaterial minds dwell in our material selves and, together, the two make a complete human. Neither can live and move and have its being independent of the other.

From Plato to the present day, the mind/body riddle has remained unanswered. If the mind is not made of matter, how can it exist? But how can one raise this question or any other without employing the mind? Today, even as the remarkable work of mapping the brain advances like never before, we still cannot tell what our minds are made of. It remains undiscovered, over the horizon, beyond reach.

To solve this problem, philosophers and scientists have usually taken one of two approaches. The first, called monism (meaning 'one-ism'), says that the body and the mind are the same thing; the mind is identical to the working brain. But beyond this point, monists divide into several camps. At one extreme, some say the brain is what really matters and the mind is no more than a sort of symptom of the physical interaction of its billions of neurons. The brain performs neurochemical and electrical functions, and the mind is a by-product of this work. At the other extreme, some say that exactly the opposite is true – the mind is real and creates everything else, including the brain, as a by-product. The entire cosmos, they say, could be the product of the mind. Creepily, the arguments for each viewpoint are often mirror images.

The second school of thought is called dualism and, as you would expect, holds that the mind and the body are not identical. Instead, no matter how intimately they function in and through each other, the mind and the brain are somehow forever different and separate. Some dualists used to hold that the mind and the brain both occupied the cranium, one made of matter and the other of an immaterial something. Most dualists now say that the brain somehow gives rise to the mind, but though the mind cannot exist apart from the brain, the mind is nevertheless fundamentally different. You can examine the matter of the brain forever, but you will not thereby examine the mind.

Inner Self and Inner Conviction

How does all this bear on the atheist's conclusion that God does not exist? The problem for naturalists is that, using the best scientific tools at hand, they have to date failed, like everyone else in human history, to get a grasp on what the mind is. They inspect brain tissue and brain function, but what the mind is remains a fundamental mystery. Meanwhile, the mind somehow keeps guiding the body to go forth through the natural world and reshape it to human ends. More broadly, we may call this inner mystery our inner selves. The inner selves of all humans direct the hands of humankind to construct human civilization. This is how the immaterial mind, the immaterial inner self, contacts the outward, natural world. And it is in and with the mysterious inner self that people keep encountering God.

The Inner Self and Faith

Naturalists apply the tools of naturalism to the inner self's convictions and find them a mixed bag – some are true, some are mistaken, some are symptoms of madness, with belief in God being mistaken or mad. But despite all reasoning, billions remain firmly convinced of God's reality. Why? Julian Baggini, a naturalist philosopher, thoughtfully observes:

> ... it seems that most religious believers justify their faith by an inner conviction... The leading Christian philosopher of religion, Alvin Plantinga, calls this faith, understood as 'a special source of knowledge, knowledge that can't be arrived at by way of reason alone'.[3]

He continues with a perceptive, even generous description of what he imagines faith to be:

> Descartes famously said that the one thing he could not doubt was the existence of his own self. Many would agree with him, with the consequence that no rational argument against the existence of the self could shake the basic conviction we have of our own existence. Skepticism dissolves when confronted with the phenomenological certainty – the indubitable feeling – of our own existence. For many religious believers, the belief in God's existence is of comparable strength. They feel the truth of God's existence so strongly that they can no more doubt it than they can doubt the existence of their own selves.

Hereafter, he warns that relying on inner conviction alone is extremely risky and then, for those who cannot imagine doubting, he piles on good reasons to 'try a little harder'. But what if a believer's inner conviction that God exists is more than a 'feeling'? What if it is actually like or even the same as his inner conviction of his own existence? And what if no other inner conviction shares this powerful status? What if this experience is deeper than the Art experience, the Love experience, or even the Beauty of Science experience? Then the argument for God becomes as powerful as the argument for the self. Granted, this is not a rational argument or even an argument at all. It is the assertion that the conviction of God's existence, there inside the inner self, goes as deep as the self, and is as real as the self.

Faith: Another Word for Relationship

The conviction of the inner self that God exists is a serviceable definition of faith. But the monotheistic faiths go further. For Jews, Christians and Muslims, the perception that God exists includes the perception that God is a person. This is the key to understanding the monotheistic experience of faith. One who has faith in a personal God may enter into a relationship with God – person to Person, self to Self.

For an atheist, this may seem strange indeed, but from the believer's standpoint, it works like the faith in other people that is common to us all. Continued and expanding faith is built on the character, commitment and open-heartedness of each party. God is a person and is known person-to-person. He is known in relationships, as the scriptures of monotheism attest. For example, the Bible goes to great lengths to describe and recall the covenants – the formal relationships – that God establishes with Israel. And when God does miraculous things for Israel, he does so for the sake of his relationship to them. This is one of the most important unifying themes of the Bible: God makes humans for relationships with him and each other.

God is Spirit

Naturalists conclude that God does not exist because he cannot be located anywhere in the natural world. Theists conclude that God transcends nature and is not subject to naturalist proofs. Neither is he subject to historical, theological, philosophical or any other kind of inspection. God is an impenetrable mystery who can be known only if he chooses to reveal himself. And such revelation, say the three monotheistic faiths, he does personally. Further, when he encounters a person, it is a spiritual encounter – God is spirit and humans are made in God's image. Jesus puts it succinctly in the Gospel of John (4:24) when he says that 'God is spirit, and his worshippers must worship in spirit and in truth.'

So what is 'spirit'? In the New Testament, the word is used to translate a Greek word that means 'breath', 'breeze' or 'wind'. 'Spirit' is used the same way in the Hebrew Bible (the Christian 'Old Testament') – it translates the Hebrew word for 'breath'. Moreover, in the Hebrew Bible, 'spirit' is also synonymous with 'life'. This is never clearer than in the very beginning of the Hebrew Bible, where the 'Spirit' in question is that of God himself and is the brooding power that calls everything into being:

> Now the earth was formless and empty, darkness was over the surface of the deep, and the Spirit of God was hovering over the waters. And God said, 'Let there be light,' and there was light (Genesis 1:2–3).

The same vital relationship of 'spirit' and 'life' is at work when God creates his masterwork, the first human:

> … the Lord God formed the man from the dust of the ground and breathed into his nostrils the breath of life, and the man became a living being (Genesis 2:7).

In short, to say 'God is spirit' is to say that God is like the wind – invisible yet near, sometimes a touch and sometimes a storm. 'God is spirit' also means that God is like the breath that powers spoken words – and when the words are God's, they call all creation into being. Finally, 'God is spirit' means that God is like the breath that moves in and out of living creatures – and this is the living breath that God breathes into mankind in particular.

The Genesis story assumes a world that is more than material. It declares that God is spirit and person, and humans, created in his image, are likewise spiritual and personal. In short, humans encounter God in the heart, the soul, the mind – the inner self, that mysterious someone, something and someplace that naturalists, along with everyone else, have yet to wrap their minds around.

CHAPTER 3

Nontheisms: No Self, No God

There is debate about whether two of the world's great religions are actually religions. Hinduism and Buddhism might better be described as philosophies, at least by Westerners who approach them with monotheistic assumptions. Then again, Hinduism and Buddhism may not be philosophies either, since both would insist that philosophy is wholly inadequate for reaching the truth about reality. So, if they are not religions and not philosophies, then what are they?

In a word, they are disciplines – teachings and methods that form a path leading to the transforming experience of seeing reality as it is. Hindus describe this experience as union with the One. Buddhists call it 'waking up'. When at last you attain it, you are freed from the roiling, death-ridden dream of reality created by the self and its cravings. Like a person rising from sleep, you shed your dreaming, isolated self, assume your true, universal Self and live no longer in dreams but in Reality.

Yet Hinduism and Buddhism contain important elements of religion that are not found in philosophy – for instance, the Hindu practice of devotion to the gods and the Buddhist practice of meditation. So it is reasonable to describe Hinduism and Buddhism as religions, though the label should be applied lightly.

The Beginnings

Hinduism and Buddhism share a strong family resemblance. And no wonder, since both, despite their own great antiquity, were born of the still more ancient traditions that today are called Vedic religion.

As early as 5000 BCE, the currents of Vedic religion emerged in India and expanded for millennia to come. During the time of the great civilization known as the Vedic Period (1500–500 BCE), the ceremonial hymns and oral traditions of Vedic religion were gathered together and written down, becoming the sacred texts known today as the Vedas. In the Vedas a reader finds something of the polytheism that thrived at the same time in the Middle East. But beneath a vast array of gods, tales of their exploits and worship of this pantheon, the Vedas offer a deeper vision. And from these Vedic roots both Hinduism and Buddhism drew their three most fundamental ideas – the Absolute One, rebirth and karma.

The Absolute Reality

The One is the ineffable Absolute that is the Reality behind all reality. It is the true source and substance of everything. Most importantly, the Absolute is the true reality of the self, the individual 'I' that each person feels him- or herself to be. Consequently, the real state of the self is utterly different from what it appears to be. In reality, none of us is a little ego with its cravings. Rather, we are in and of the Infinite One. When we realize this union personally, we gain complete freedom. This is freedom from self and its futile attachments to every passing thing. This is freedom from all illusion, a freedom far beyond anything the blind ego can imagine, for it includes freedom from the illusion of ego itself, along with its cravings that keep us suffering through life. In Hinduism, the Absolute is named Brahman.

Rebirth and Karma

Vedic religion also gives to Hinduism and Buddhism two other essential and closely related ideas – rebirth and karma.

The first declares that the grip of ego can imprison one not only through an entire lifetime, but also through death itself and into rebirth in a succeeding life. This endless cycle of life upon life, suffering upon suffering, death upon death, is the Wheel of Rebirth, the great cycle that traps everyone. We return in succeeding lives because of karma, the law of just consequences for the life you have lived.

How one lives could never be ignored. In the Vedic period, right living was recognized as a crucial element of the greater Right Order found through all of nature. The entire balance of creation was affected when people failed to rightly order their own lives. As a result, organizing each person's duties became an important function within Vedic religion. From this concern with order eventually arose the caste system, which placed each person in one of many possible stations in the larger order of things. In this role a man attended to his proper duties, his right behaviour, and thereby accumulated good karma that would eventually place him in a higher station in a life to come. In time, a man could rise to the highest caste of Brahmin and, from there, find union with the Absolute. By the way, note that Brahmin is one of three words with a common origin but very different meanings: Brah*man* is the Absolute, Brah*min* is a social class and Brah*ma* is the name of a god who is one manifestation of the Absolute.

The law of karma is inexorably, absolutely just. Live rightly and you will accrue good karma, which elevates you in your next life. Continue to live rightly in successive lives and your good karma will raise you in the human order until you attain enlightenment, union with the One, and the end of rebirth. On the other hand, should you live wrongly, your bad karma will consign you to reincarnation as a lower rank of man or even a lower form of creature. Not until you live rightly will the law of karma permit you to rise to eventual union with the One.

The One, the Wheel of Rebirth, and karma – these are the great creations of Vedic religion that also become the foundations of Hinduism and Buddhism.

The Dilemma of Vedic Religion

For all its greatness, Vedic religion was insufficient to answer a profound question: if right living is the way to union with the One, then how can anyone attain it? After all, who in her heart of hearts is righteous? Who can claim to be perfectly just and no longer subject to the law of just consequences? Who can escape the Wheel of Rebirth? These were the questions that gave rise to a new understanding of the One and man's relationship to it. This new understanding was the beginning of Hinduism.

Hinduism: Release from Rebirth

Hinduism arose with a solution to the problem of inescapable karma and inevitable rebirth. The way of escape, early Hindu gurus taught, comes through the mystical realization of oneness with the Absolute. With this realization comes liberation from the cycle of rebirth and re-death. The path to liberation is demanding, but when a person at last attains it, he is forever transformed. He sees through all illusion and at last beholds things as they really are. Most of all, he sees himself as he is – no longer an isolated, struggling ego, but now in union with the One Reality and living in the blissful unity of the Absolute.

The Rise of Hinduism

As it rose from Vedic religion, Hinduism reshaped it by gathering up its myriad divinities and even the One into a greater Reality behind all things, now called Brahman. The gods still have their role, but in Hinduism they are ultimately manifestations of Brahman – the Eternal, the Pure Consciousness, the unfathomable Source of Being.

In Hinduism, Brahman becomes more accessible to humans, more willing to accommodate their limitations. Now Brahman is revealed in three different, yet intimately related, divine persons: Brahma (no final 'n') is the Creator; Vishnu is the Sustainer; and Shiva is the Destroyer who prepares the world for its rebirth. Beneath Brahman, the One manifested in three divinities, is the vast host of gods who fill the Hindu pantheon – 30,000 by some counts, while others put the number at 330 million. Worship of the gods has an important place in Hindu life, but union with Brahman comes by a practice or 'yoga' – any of four disciplines in meditation, contemplation and action.

Four Paths to Brahman

Of the four practices that lead to union with Brahman, the most popular is the Way of Devotion (Bhakti Yoga), the path of loving God. For the more contemplative devotee, the Way of Meditation (Dhyana Yoga) can lead to the apprehension of Brahman. For others, the Way of Works (Karma Yoga) turns daily life and duty into a path to Brahman. Worshippers may also journey via the Way of Knowledge (Jnana Yoga) and its disciplined regimen of study. But whatever the Way, the goal is the same – release from the Wheel of Rebirth through union with Brahman.

These methods can help anyone to find a way to Brahman. The worshipful Hindu may also find more help in wholehearted devotion to a chosen deity, all of whom are ultimately icons and manifestations of Brahman. Worship of the gods is widespread among Hindus, who regard all gods, including the God of monotheistic faiths, as manifestations of Brahman.

The Broad Sweep of Hinduism

In the same way that Vedic religion was endlessly diverse, Hinduism has always been a broad river. Hinduism resists centralized authority – with interesting results. Unlike Catholic and Eastern Christianity, Hinduism has no authoritative prelates or councils to rule on doctrinal issues. Instead, there is plenty of room for divergent and even conflicting ideas to coexist. No one worries overmuch about consistency.

For instance, one strain of Hindu tradition has made room for the dualistic belief that spirit is superior to matter, which forms a prison that keeps spirit entrapped. Therefore, the task of the devout person is to undertake the deep introspection that will liberate his individual spirit from his material body.

But another current within Hinduism has rejected dualism and asserts that spirit is the one and only reality. Matter is not a prison – it is an illusion. Through the proper yogic practice one can awaken from this dream and experience release from rebirth.

These and other important variations within Hinduism illustrate its creative breadth, from which, in time, there arose entirely new faiths – including Jainism, Sikhism and, most importantly, Buddhism.

Hinduism Today

About 900 million people worldwide are Hindus, and the great majority live in India and its northern neighbour, Nepal. Within Hinduism, diversity of belief is breathtaking, covering the spectrum from monotheism, to polytheism, to pantheism, to monism, to atheism.

But however many varying elements Hinduism embraces, the majority of Hindus believe in this foundational truth: within every person, beyond the ego, there lives the true Self, the eternal soul called 'atman', the spirit that is shared by every human and is united with infinite Brahman. The goal of life is to realize that one's atman is one with Brahman and, seeing this transforming truth, to enter into freedom from rebirth.

At the same time, a sizeable minority of other schools within Hinduism perceive Brahman as the Supreme Personal Being. Every human's atman depends wholly on this God, and by God's grace comes escape from the self and oneness with all. This God is even called 'the Lord'. He sounds personal enough to be familiar to monotheists, but the Hindu Lord is very different. He is associated with other divinities, including Brahma, Vishnu and Shiva, and, depending on what strain of Hinduism is under discussion, he may be regarded with everything from non-belief to the conviction that this personal God is identical with Brahman, the Infinite Principle.

The daily life of worship and observance for Hindus is just as various. Practices can include: ritual bathing throughout the day; worship at the family's shrine at home, which includes lighting candles and offering foods before images of the gods; reciting scriptures, chanting, singing hymns and more. These can all vary by region, village and the personal preferences of individuals. Pilgrimages and festivals are abundant and year-round.

Of some interest to Westerners is Hinduism's veneration of cows. This has its roots in early history, when people depended on cows for the essentials of life – food, field labour and fertilizer. Today the cow is a symbol of selfless giving and, in a religion that also prizes vegetarianism, the idea of eating beef is repugnant.

Buddhism: A New Way to the One

By the sixth century BCE, Hinduism was for many no longer the way of liberation it had once been. Union with Brahman had come to involve practices so demanding that only monks, the full-time religious practitioners, could hope to accomplish them. For common followers, burdened with daily life, the task was too difficult. It was inevitable that pressure for reform began to mount.

That reform arrived in the shape of a man named Siddhartha Gautama (around 560–480 BCE). Siddhartha was born a prince whose royal father was determined to keep him away from a religious destiny by making life within the palace too glorious to forsake. Every privilege of wealth and power was bestowed on the young man, who drank in all of them. But a few trips beyond the palace walls were sufficient to show him the sobering truth about the rest of the world. Here he was struck by what Buddhists call the Four Sights – a man burdened by disease, another crushed by age and another stilled by death. The last of the Four Sights was an ascetic. Deeply moved and disturbed by these sights, Siddhartha eventually determined to leave his life of privilege and, like the ascetic, search for a higher existence. In fact, he began a quest for nothing less than freedom from suffering and death.

For the next six years, he worked with full devotion. He spent time with holy men who advocated strenuous teachings and yogic practices, but none of this solved life's deepest problems. He spent more years among the ascetics, practising self-denial with such focus he nearly starved himself to death. But in the end, this path also led nowhere.

Siddhartha Becomes the Buddha

Finally, having forsaken all these efforts, he seated himself beneath a tree and vowed to remain there until he found the path to freedom. It was there that Siddhartha, meditating deeply and finally defeating the spirit of ignorance and death, attained enlightenment and complete freedom. He became the Buddha, the Enlightened One.

Thereafter, Buddha journeyed and taught his message of escape from suffering and death through enlightenment. It soon became clear that this message was something distinct from traditional Hindu teachings, and in time it established itself as the path now known as Buddhism.

But what was this new message of enlightenment? Remarkably, the Buddha's teaching is easy to summarize. In fact, the basic tenets of Buddhism are fully captured in two well-known formulations: the Four Noble Truths and the Eightfold Path.

The Four Noble Truths are a straightforward definition of mankind's problem:

1. *The human problem* is that we suffer.
2. *The cause* of our suffering is our craving.
3. *Craving and suffering* actually can cease.
4. *To achieve cessation,* follow the Eightfold Path.

Once a follower takes these four truths deeply to heart, she is ready to set out on the way of escape via the Eightfold Path. The name of each step is translated differently by different writers, but those suggested by Dr Jeffrey Webb,[4] Professor of History at Huntington College in Indiana, reveal the relationship of each step to the next:

1. *Right Views.* Our instinctive view of ourselves as the autonomous, in-charge, centre of things only leads to more suffering. A right view of existence, one that leads to freedom from death, takes the self off the throne.
2. *Right Intent.* It is right to see our self-obsession, but we must also want to change. We must want to leave self-absorption behind.
3. *Right Speech.* When we talk to others, the selfish ego expresses and exposes itself. We should shed it by simply speaking the truth. No more verbal abuse, no more lies – and no more half-truths, coercions or other manipulations.
4. *Right Conduct.* From the preceding steps, the action we take will change. As we leave behind the self and its self-seeking, we cease from harming others and begin to act with compassion.
5. *Right Livelihood.* Your right conduct will extend to your profession. Does it require a selfish ego that harms others? If so, you should cease your old ways and find a profession that provides for you and helps the well-being of others.
6. *Right Effort.* Now that your outward life is coming right, you can better discipline your inward life to do likewise. Discipline the mind to cease from mental states that are

focused on the ego. Bring the mind to focus on the limitless Reality all around.

7.   *Right Mindfulness*. Now go even deeper. Undertake the deep meditation that uncovers the buried connections between our passions and the hidden manipulations of the ego. When the deepest workings of the ego are found, you can cease from them and approach final enlightenment.

8.   *Right Concentration*. The goal lies just ahead. Through systematic meditation, you go beyond the ego entirely, beyond all its creations of thought and feeling, beyond illusion, beyond mental states altogether. You finally shed the consciousness of the self, the ego, and see Reality directly. You pass from self-consciousness and enter into a direct, personal comprehension of the Absolute. You leave behind suffering and death. You attain Nirvana.

Nirvana, Not Brahman

The parallels between Hinduism and Buddhism show just how closely they are related. But it is important to know what separated Buddhism from its Hindu beginnings. Most importantly, Nirvana is not the same as Brahman. Brahman is the great One in which all things are one. Some great Hindu traditions think of the One as impersonal while others see it as personal and God-like, but the Buddhist idea of Nirvana is different from both. It is the state of cessation – the word Nirvana itself comes from roots that mean 'extinguish'.

What is extinguished is our egoistic grasping after illusions. We finally shed all desire to grasp what we can never hold, namely, a world so changeable and impermanent that it is less than smoke, less than a dream. Everything is impermanent, in flux, and nothing exists of itself. Everything is dependent, arising from something else, from 'causes' and 'conditions' in a cycle rooted in ignorance and craving. And when we shed all attachments, we shed the ego itself – and finally, we discover our true identity and the true Reality that was hidden by illusion. When we shed our entanglement in the vast, shimmering panorama of illusion, we awaken. The ego is extinguished and we are free to enter Nirvana, that new and blissful Reality, free of illusion, free of suffering and death, free of the bondage of existence driven by the ego. This is the bliss of non-existence.

Reincarnation

Buddha also changed the way people understand reincarnation. In opposition to Hinduism, Buddha taught that the soul is just one more illusion of attachment and has no real existence. Yet the Wheel of Rebirth turns and reincarnation is always at work. What, then, is reincarnated if not the soul? Buddha held that, for those still entangled with the illusory ego, an illusion of self proceeds through successive reincarnated lives, but is no more individual or substantive than an ephemeral flame that is transmitted from candle to candle. When a 'soul', burdened by reincarnation into life after life, finally realizes that it is a self bound up in illusion, it ceases to exist, and the true person attains Nirvana.

That has important implications for the idea of karma, the law of just consequences. For the Buddhist, karma isn't really workable, either, since the soul is an illusion. Buddhists explain that karma works on the five insubstantial threads, called 'skandas', from which our lives are woven. Karma may influence them, but skandas share in the illusory nature of all existence, leaving karma powerless to bind our true selves with consequences that must be worked out in lives to come. Therefore, astoundingly and in opposition to Hinduism, we do not have to pass through many lives and rise through the caste system to reach freedom. A person can reach awakening in this life, here and now.

The Varieties of Buddhism

Like the Hinduism from which it stems, Buddhism is a broad river. But among its many variations, several are most widely practised. The oldest of these is Theravada Buddhism, which became organized around the monks who were the keepers of Buddhist practice and tradition. Their Buddhism became so rigorous that it began to shut out commoners, the very people whom the monks relied upon for the donations that sustained them. As ever, exclusivity gave rise to reform, in this case creating the new movement known as Mahayana Buddhism, which broadened the field of those who could reach Nirvana. In turn, Mahayana became the parent of other major Buddhist traditions, most notably Tibetan and Zen Buddhism. Though these strains have many differences, all find a common foundation in the pillars of faith known as the Three Jewels.

The Three Jewels
The first jewel is the Buddha himself. He is indispensable to Buddhism because he discovered the path to freedom and, even more, postponed his final entry into Nirvana in order to teach the path to others. His great work is now interpreted and understood in a wide variety of ways, but beneath them all is the Buddha himself.

The second jewel is the Dharma, the proper teaching that keeps one firmly on the path to Nirvana. These teachings were written down and elaborated into a collection of scriptures far larger than those found in other major religions.

Buddhism's third jewel is the Sangha, the community of those who follow Buddha. Their experience and wisdom also guide the follower along the right path.

However much they may vary on how to interpret the Three Jewels, Buddhists of all strains rely on them for strength and truth.

Hinduism, Buddhism and God
There are differences so profound between Hinduism, Buddhism and the three main monotheistic faiths – Judaism, Christianity and

Islam – that they seem to have little to say to each other. But there are also harmonizing themes, at least, by which they enlighten each other.

From any perspective, the deepest difference concerns God. Simply put, neither Hindus nor Buddhists think in terms of anything like the one God of monotheism. Instead of God, Hindus and Buddhists discover the object of revelation to be the Absolute or, for Buddhists, plain Reality as it truly is. Instead of encountering a supernatural person, the Hindu or Buddhist experiences enlightenment and escapes from suffering, death and rebirth.

Buddhism in particular holds that God is not a helpful idea. When asked about God, Buddha was silent, perhaps indicating that God was just another creation of the self, an illusion and a distraction. Hindus, on the other hand, may worship a heaven full of gods, but ultimately understand them as icons of the ultimate, inconceivable One.

Ultimate Reality vs Ultimate Relationship

By contrast, instead of seeking ultimate enlightenment, monotheists are looking for the ultimate relationship. That is why the Bible, for instance, is full of stories about humankind's closeness to and estrangement from God. What is at stake is a relationship and not a philosophical or mystical revelation.

The greatest hope of monotheism is perfect relationship with God – and its greatest desolation is that relationship violated. In the Bible, the violation of relationship with God is named 'sin', a word that always implies relationship. One can sin not only against God but also against fellow humans. A useful synonym for sin is 'betrayal'.

Therefore, in Judaism, Christianity and Islam, the chief problem is sin – a broken relationship with God. Its consequences are alienation from God, from other people and from the creation itself. In the end, alienation from God means death.

But in Hinduism and Buddhism, the problem of mankind is the ego's attachment to the illusory world. This is what causes suffering and death and what must be 'solved' if we are to escape them. Here the solution to suffering and death is enlightenment. Furthermore, Hindus and Buddhists need no redemption from beyond the self by God or Jesus or Allah or anyone else. All that is needed to gain escape from suffering and death is already within the follower. She need only awaken to gain enlightenment.

Deeper Than the Mind

From a Christian perspective, the Buddhist idea of 'awakening' deeply misunderstands the world. The creation story in Genesis offers just one of many biblical declarations that neither the world nor the self is illusory. They are definitely real and definitely good. But when mankind betrays its relationship with God, the creation and mankind both become broken, fallen into suffering and death.

Moreover, this fall is fatal. God is life itself, so separation from God is the exhaustive, final definition of death. Unless God comes to mankind, the self cannot live again. It cannot awaken from death on its own. And that is why, to the Christian, Buddhism's central experience of waking from all illusion, including the illusion of death, seems to be only more illusion.

The Common Ground of Compassion

Yet an 'awake' Buddhist should brim naturally with compassion, as Buddha did. For Christianity and Judaism, compassion is also the pinnacle and evidence of true belief – love of God and love of one's neighbour as oneself. Presumably, then, if an enlightened Buddhist, a devout Jew and a dedicated Christian were all neighbours, each would love the others as himself.

And how then would an observer tell their religions apart?

CHAPTER 4

Polytheism and Pantheism: The God-filled Universe

Preliterate people were also pre-theological. This is not to say that they were ignorant or unthinking when it came to the Divine. In fact, just the opposite was true. But rather than formulating carefully rationalized understandings of God, they explored the meaning of the Divine through the use of stories. Stories gave early people the means to talk about the great mysteries of life and death, the earth and the heavens, time and eternity.

Many of their greatest stories, which we now call myths, survive to this day, showing us how ancient people understood the cosmos and their place in it. But just for the record, it is important to distinguish between the two modern meanings of the word 'myth'. In the most common usage, a myth is any sort of fabrication or fiction, as in 'the Loch Ness monster does not exist; it is a myth, no more real than, say, the Loch Ness Flying Pig'. But in the second usage, a myth is something else entirely. It is a traditional story that explains a people's belief about the world. A myth in this sense is not concerned with historical or scientific truths because it aims to tell different, more important truths – for example, that the entire creation is good, that people are born of the earth, that the ocean is a power too vast to tame.

Myth and Gods

So 'myth' can mean two entirely different things. But in this discussion, it means one thing only – the great stories by which people explain to themselves the creation and their place in it. And when we look at myths, we find them filled with gods.

For example, 3,000 years ago, for the people in the region that now includes Iraq, the myth of the god Marduk's victory over Tiamat explained how the world came to be. When Marduk overcame the primal god Tiamat in war, he cut her dead body in two; from one half came the sky, from the other, the earth. In Egypt, the world came to be when Atum arose from the vast, watery chaos and created the gods of air and moisture. These in turn gave birth to sky and earth, and, ultimately, from their divine offspring came fertile land and life.

Similarly, the stories of the ancient Greek gods emerged to organize and explain the creation. From Chaos, the great unformed void that preceded everything, came Gaia (the earth); from Gaia came Uranus (the sky); and together they gave birth to a host of other gods. These clashed in cosmic struggles and coupled in myriad ways to birth even more gods, all of whom eventually came under the rule of Zeus. Zeus himself fathered still more gods and demigods to fill out the vast Greek pantheon.

The Gods and Nature

Common to all these myths is the connection between the gods and nature. It was the gods who ruled nature, and therefore, by engaging with the gods, one could understand and perhaps control the mystery and power of the natural world. The gods of sun, rain, fields and grains were essential allies for raising abundant crops. No wonder it became essential to honour, serve and beseech these gods. The same was true of the mysterious and untamed inner world of mankind, influenced and overshadowed by such gods as the Muses, the divine sisters who granted inspiration for the arts; the goddess Mania, the personification of insanity; Hypnos, the god of sleep, and many more.

It is from myths that these gods emerged as distinct supernatural persons, to whom humans offered worship, sacrifice and prayers – the practices at the centre of religion, practices that help distinguish religion from its purely mythic roots.

Everywhere in the ancient world, polytheism was the norm. But of course, there was no united and uniform polytheistic system of belief. In fact, the malleability of polytheism was and remains one of its hallmarks. Gods and demigods easily migrated between cultures and their pantheons, as the case of the Roman gods makes abundantly clear. As the Roman empire spread, it made a point of adopting the gods of its newly conquered nations, and, eventually, as the Romans took over the lands of the former Greek empire, they absorbed Greek gods wholesale, along with Greek culture. The Greek god Dionysus became the Roman god Bacchus; Eros became Cupid; Zeus became Jupiter; Heracles became Hercules, and so on. The Roman pantheon swelled with immigrant Greek divinity.

Meanwhile in India a universe of Hindu gods thrived, serving as the countless manifestations of Brahman. Today, from their vast pantheon Hindus worship any gods they choose, though their choices have much to do with their family and region, so it is unsurprising that the Hindu calendar bulges with days devoted to celebrating the gods.

Hinduism is surely the best known of modern polytheistic religions, if one remembers to add that Hindu belief ultimately leads one to Brahman. Even so, the daily life of Hindus involves devotion to their chosen god or gods and includes prayer before a representation of the god, offerings of food and more. To a monotheist, this looks like polytheism, pure and simple. To a Hindu, it looks pure but not simple, reflecting as it does the great, inclusive sweep of Hindu belief.

Hinduism is polytheistic, monotheistic, non-theistic and even atheistic, depending on which strain of Hinduism one examines. But even setting aside its non-polytheistic branches, Hinduism is still the largest of today's polytheistic religions.

Yet Hinduism is also the world's largest pantheistic religion. How can a religion be both polytheistic and pantheistic? By living with tension. The pantheist strain wants to absorb all gods into Brahman, the One. The polytheist current wants to retain and worship the gods by the million. In the end, Hinduism insists that both views must coexist and, together, express a greater truth – the One is all and the gods reveal the million facets of that Oneness.

All is God

Pantheism, however, can be found standing on its own, unencumbered by additional '-isms', from the time of the Presocratic Greek philosophers in the sixth century BCE, up to our own day. The word 'pantheism' explains itself: 'pan-' means 'all' and 'the-' (from *theo*) means 'God'. So a sturdy working definition of pantheism is that all is God.

That leads to two reasonable but problematic conclusions. First, pantheism holds that the material universe is equivalent to God. But the second conclusion is the difficulty: if the material universe is God, then why complicate things by naming it God? Why not just call it the Universe and leave it at that? That would make pantheism just another name for naturalism, the belief that the natural world is the only reality. And that is exactly the criticism that naturalists have levelled against pantheism for centuries. Pantheism, they say, is needlessly dressed up with meaningless God-talk and is, at bottom, naturalism.

But most pantheists protest because they insist on two very important additions to their definition of pantheism. They further assert that a) nature is somehow a unity and b) that unity is somehow divine.

Of course, naturalists point and jeer at the 'somehow' in this new and improved definition, but most pantheists see it as indispensable to understanding the deep and abiding truth about reality. The creation, they say, is not overseen by an external creator, but it is indeed infused with unmistakable and overwhelming magnificence. Nature is so exalted that the right response is to call it holy. To see a desert sky at midnight or a mountain range in the morning is to experience that glory, personally and directly, and offer back a reverence as deep as worship.

Not surprisingly, naturalists still want to know how pantheists can use words like 'holy' and 'sacred' of what is, in the end, simply nature. Pantheists mostly respond with a shrug and say they feel it, heart and soul.

A Philosopher of Pantheism

If that seems too subjective, then turn to the seventeenth-century philosopher Baruch Spinoza (1632–77) for a more grounded pantheism. He felt the holy so deeply in nature that others called him 'god-intoxicated', yet he grounded his pantheism in a rationalist system that philosophers still regard as beautiful and important. He put forth a deeply reasoned claim that 'God' and 'Nature' are two names for a single, unitary 'Substance'. This Substance is far greater than what we conventionally label as matter, mind and even God. Spinoza's Substance is the unity that underlies everything and makes all of it subject to the same laws – unified laws that rule all of reality in the realm of matter and the realm of thought.

Immediately, Spinoza was rightly understood to be a pantheist and wrongly hounded for it. Public opprobrium eventually forced him into a silence that kept much of his important work out of publication until after his death.

But his pantheism has lived on. His 'God or Nature' was sufficiently spiritual to provide an alternative to materialistic atheism. At the same time, his 'God or Nature' was present in daily existence – and far more appealing than the impersonal First Cause that earlier philosophers declared to be the indispensable start of the created order.

Einstein put great stock in Spinoza, writing in 1929 that 'I believe in Spinoza's God who reveals himself in the orderly harmony of what exists, not in a God who concerns himself with the fates and actions of human beings.' Twentieth-century leftist and Marxist philosophy drew on Spinoza as well, along with great writers such as Jorge Luis Borges. Today, Spinoza's idea of the underlying unity of both creation and consciousness finds itself at home among many philosophers of ecology as well.

The New Pagans

Spinoza's pantheism is also fully compatible with the contemporary movement known as neopaganism. But neopagans are just as likely to be polytheists, monotheists, dualists or several other sorts of '-theists' because the new pagans draw their beliefs from so many sources. These include the religious mythologies of Norse, Celtic, Roman, Egyptian and other ancient cultures; the folklore of these same cultures; modern sciences; Buddhism, Christianity and other living religions; ecological and feminist philosophy; and as many other sources as this eclectic spirituality cares to employ.

Perhaps the best known of neopagan religions is Wicca, with its emphasis on female spirituality and empowerment. Other new faiths include Asatru (Norse paganism), Druidism (Celtic paganism) and Goddess worship.

But generally, a common current runs through all of neopaganism: a dissatisfaction with the spiritual poverty of mainstream modern religions, their hierarchies and authoritarianism, and their hopeless entanglement with the evils of modernity – the power of the wealthy and the plunder of creation. Neopagans long to shed all this and regain the vitality of the Old Ways, the religions that placed man within nature, not above it, and animated the heavens and earth with spirits and Spirit.

But neopaganism's claims to historicity are a mixed bag. Some parts of it do indeed labour to recapture an ancient paganism, while other wings adapt mythologies to suit their own tastes, and still others rely on purported history actually dreamed up in the twentieth century. Important parts of Wicca, for example, rely on the deeply problematic works of Margaret Murray from the 1920s and of Gerald Gardner from 1939 to 1959.

Furthermore, any serious return to the Old Ways must face their dark side. From China, to the Middle East, to Europe, to the New World, ancient polytheistic religions practised human sacrifice to appease the wrath and gain the favour of the gods. Methods included hanging, drowning, stabbing, live evisceration, live incineration and live burial. Victims included prisoners, slaves, women, children and babies. Polytheistic paganism also practised ritual prostitution employing women, girls and boys. Unsurprisingly, given these horrific means of gaining the gods' attentions, fear of local gods was another prominent feature of pagan religions. Even today, traces of that fear persist in our language – the meaning of our word 'panic' is rooted in the shattering terror one feels at the presence of Pan, the god of wild places.

Of course, when polytheistic paganism flourished, wild places were nearly the whole of nature, and, while we moderns may get our impressions of the natural world from national forests and municipal parks, ancient polytheists lived daily in a nature that, though beautiful, was limitlessly powerful and relentlessly dangerous. Humans were so much a part of nature that they suffered continually under its arbitrary dictates of plague, drought, flood, fire, famine and other cruelties. Small wonder that pagans believed the gods required lavish and bloody appeasement rather than, say, an hour of casual thanks at the solstices.

All this is in stark contrast to the romanticism of neopaganism, which prefers a kindly and personal nature and a humanity that, though at times misguided, is well able to harmonize itself with creation. In the neopagan world, the problem of evil is a family secret that people would rather not talk about.

Despite all these cracks in its foundations, neopaganism has established a small beachhead of about one million adherents worldwide.[5] But for our purposes, the importance of neopaganism is not in its numbers, but in the breadth of its conception of God. If you thought that polytheism and pantheism in the Western world were long gone, consider a possible comeback of the old pantheon via neopaganism.

Christian Pantheism?

Oddly enough, another upwelling of modern pantheism can be found in the writings of John Shelby Spong, a retired bishop of the American Episcopal Church. Depending on whom you talk to, his ideas are either inspired or heretical, inasmuch as they call for the central doctrines of historical Christianity to be dumped entirely and replaced with a naturalistic, pantheistic interpretation of God.

The New Luther

A succinct version of his programme is found in his 1998 document entitled 'A Call for a New Reformation'. Here he invokes Luther's Ninety-five Theses, the document that fully unleashed the Reformation, and offers an analysis of modern history and the fatal ways in which Christianity has been unable to evolve with it. Finally, he presents his own Twelve Theses as the foundation for the new reformation that will 'dwarf' the old one in intensity.

In brief, he asserts that the Reformation failed to grapple with 'the basic and identifying marks of Christianity itself',[6] a change demanded by the march of history and of science in particular. Copernicus and Galileo, Sir Isaac Newton, Darwin and Freud have made it impossible for the essence of Christianity to survive in its current form – a pre-modern mythology filled with a sky-father, miracles, sin, salvation, resurrection and a future utopia. A total revolution must now erupt, one that begins at the heart of the matter – the Christian definition of God.

The New God

Spong declares that 'God can no longer be conceived in theistic terms',[7] monotheistic or otherwise. Take a close look at the old, traditional God, he says, the God of the Old Testament and of Christian history, and one can only conclude that he is a human creation, a wish-fulfilling projection of the human self to cosmic proportions, as Freud in particular establishes. This is the now bankrupt 'theistic' idea of God.

All of which has enormous implications for the person of Jesus. He cannot be the son of a god who does not exist. His death cannot be a sacrifice for sin – a 'barbarian idea'.[8] And his physical resurrection and ascension must be discarded as nothing more than pre-scientific superstition.

Even though the theistic God must be abandoned, Spong cannot abandon his powerful inner 'experience of something other, transcendent, and beyond all of my limits...'[9] On this basis he declares a God who is the ground of all being, who penetrates and surrounds everything, but who is not a transcendent, separate being and certainly not a person. Of course, all this is a good definition of pantheism.

Clearly, one very visible churchman has migrated to pantheism from monotheism in general and historical Christianity in particular. But his larger mission to convert all of Christianity to his own pantheism is misguided for several reasons.

Inconvenient Truths

First of all, the Bishop is a latecomer. Christianity has long considered pantheism and declared itself irreconcilable with it. Christians embodied their conclusions in creeds arising from an initial four-century struggle against a host of surrounding religions, including various pantheisms, that threatened to engulf it. In the end, the creeds clearly proclaimed a monotheistic and personal God, the divinity of Jesus Christ, his bodily resurrection and more.

Second, Spong's critique is provincial. He sees historical Christianity struggling everywhere to stay alive, but its decline is evidenced only in Western mainline denominations, including his own. Non-denominational Christianity thrives in the US and is well represented in Europe. In the rest of the world, including sub-saharan Africa, South America and even Asia, Christianity is expanding. For example, 26–49 per cent of South Koreans are now Christians,[10] and in China, Christianity continues its underground expansion despite fifty years of harsh government persecution and may now 'make up five percent of China's population, or 65 million believers'.[11]

Finally, Spong is confused about history. For example, he weighs the fundamental struggle of the Reformation – justification by faith alone (per Luther) versus justification by faith with works (per Rome) – and pronounces it 'insignificant'. But, of course, the Reformation proclamation of 'faith alone' was nothing less than a direct assault on the foundations of the Roman Church's spiritual and temporal power, vested as it was in the church's exclusive control of God's grace. 'Faith alone' was the idea that restructured the entire order of Christian faith and European polity.

Nevertheless, whatever its weaknesses, the Bishop's story exemplifies the attraction that many people feel towards the pantheist explanation of the divine impulse, the human condition and the material world. For Bishop Spong and for millions worldwide, pantheism is a living faith.

CHAPTER 5

Monotheism: One God Alone

When a Hindu befriends a Jew, a Christian and a Muslim, he welcomes all three into his temple and invites them to bring their God with them. For Hindus, it is self-evident that anyone else's God can take a place in their polytheist pantheon and that all faiths may worship together, each focusing on the god(s) of its choice. All gods are ways to encounter Brahman, the great One in which all reality exists, so any and every god is honoured – Vishnu, Yahweh, Shiva, Jesus, the goddess Lakshmi, Allah and millions more are all paths to the Ultimate.

But if they are orthodox, the Jew, the Christian and the Muslim would recoil from the invitation, for each believes his God to be the only God. Not only is it abhorrent to think of setting him as equal among other gods, but even the existence of other gods is a false idea to monotheists. In monotheism, God is one God alone. There are no others.

The monotheist conception did not arrive overnight. From the beginning, polytheism was the norm in the ancient world, with wide arrays of gods who existed in complicated family relationships. The lesser gods would be worshipped in their various home territories, and a single, greater god was put forth as their ruler. Unsurprisingly, the chief god was also the deity most closely associated with the ruling temporal power.

The Father of Monotheism

It was in a milieu like this that the Bible set the story of Abram. Here is a man like his neighbours and his clansmen – and therefore a polytheist – who hears from a deity whose command to him will, in time, completely change the world's understanding of God. In this essential biblical story, it is God who speaks to Abram, not a local god or even the chief of the gods. God's name is Yahweh, (pronounced YAH-way) and he is God over all. His life-changing, world-changing command to Abram is this:

> The Lord had said to Abram, 'Leave your country, your people and your father's household and go to the land I will show you. I will make you into a great nation and I will bless you; I will make your name great, and you will be a blessing. I will bless those who bless you, and whoever curses you I will curse; and all peoples on earth will be blessed through you' (Genesis 12:1–3).

What makes God's command so compelling is that, to follow it, Abram must abandon everything that, in his culture, made for security. As a city dweller, living in the large, important city of Ur, Abram lived a safer, better life than that of nomadic people. That would have to be abandoned. He would also leave behind his father's household and therefore a substantial inheritance of land, livestock, workers and more – all of it the basis of wealth and well-being in ancient times. He would leave his father's clansmen and therefore the comprehensive security – social, political, economic and physical – that the clan provided. Finally, by leaving his homeland, he would leave all the gods associated with it. In short, by listening to God and doing what he asks, Abram would have to abandon completely his old life, his old gods and his old security. He would put himself entirely in Yahweh's hands.

But there is more to God's command. If he obeys, Abram will gain the immeasurable wealth of descendants beyond number, a nation that will bless every family on earth.

Abram obeys God. He packs up his own livestock, servants and property and strikes out for a new, unknown home, guided by the God who has broken into his life. Decades pass as Abram listens to God and leads his household. Then God speaks again to Abram, renewing his promise of descendants and confirming it by changing his servant's name from Abram ('exalted father') to Abraham ('father of a multitude').

In years to come, God speaks to Abraham again, bestowing promises that would, as centuries passed, shape Abraham's descendants into the nation of Israel. That history is part of the continuing story within the Jewish and Christian scriptures.

The One God

But the foundation on which this story is built is the nature and character of Abraham's God. Clearly Abraham understood the God who spoke to him to be nothing like the many gods of Abraham's father, neighbours and ancestors. He was not a local god, bound to one place. He was not one god among many, a grain god, say, or a river god. He was not even god over other gods. In the story of Abraham, God is Almighty God alone. He makes a covenant with Abraham that is unlimited by place or even by time.

It is from these beginnings that God's relationship with Abraham and his descendants unfolds as God reveals himself more and more clearly. Through centuries of obedience and disobedience, enslavement and oppression, deliverance and freedom, Israel comes to understand the nature of its god: he is the one God alone. And here at last is true monotheism.

In fact, Abraham's encounter with the one God and his promises is the foundation on which the world's great monotheistic religions stand. Judaism, Christianity and Islam all claim Abraham as their spiritual father and Abraham's God as their God.

God Against the Gods

But from the beginning and forever after, a great struggle has attended the worship of God alone. The conflict is against other gods. Through the Hebrew Bible, the battle of God against the gods runs from beginning to end, as Yahweh commands his people to turn from idolatry and seek only him.

The question is 'why?' Why is God so exercised about other gods? And what makes them so powerfully attractive to God's people? Is there any room for compromise? Could God and his people meet in the middle on this?

Definitely not. The Ten Commandments are among the Bible's greatest expressions of God's relationship to his people, mapping out how they may live in peace with him and with each other. The commandments cover relationships within the family and community, but above all, they address each person's relationship with God. The first commandment is clear:

> 'I am the Lord your God, who brought you out of Egypt, out of the land of slavery. You shall have no other gods before me' (Exodus 20:2–3).

Note that the second sentence is better translated as 'You shall have no other gods *in my face.*' Other gods are an affront and a betrayal.

God's stance becomes clear in the second commandment, which takes the issue of other gods even further:

> 'You shall not make for yourself an idol in the form of anything in heaven above or on the earth beneath or in the waters below. You shall not bow down to them or worship them; for I, the Lord your God, am a jealous God, punishing the children for the sin of the fathers to the third and fourth generation of those who hate me, but showing love to a thousand (generations) of those who love me and keep my commandments' (Exodus 20:4–6).

In the Ancient Middle East, to refer to things 'in heaven, on earth and in the waters below' was equivalent to the modern idea of 'everything in the entire universe'. The inference is that, because God is the source of all creation and the One on whom everything depends for existence, to worship any created thing is, at best, to entirely miss who God is. At worst, idol worship attempts a sort of takeover of creation – to deny God and nominate the sun, the moon, or another creature to be the source of all being. This is why God bans worship of idols and, therefore, all polytheistic worship.

Notice also that the second command goes on at some length not about idols specifically, but about those who love God and those who do not. Because these issues are set together in the same command, it reveals that those who worship idols are actually those who hate God. Note further that the text says it is they who hate God and not the other way round. At bottom, this command holds that embracing an idol is equivalent to abandoning God. One may embrace God or one may embrace idols, but there is no middle ground. To choose God is to forsake all others.

There is still more in the third commandment. It is not explicitly about other gods, as are the first and second commands, but it goes straight to the heart of the matter. It confronts the impulse to false worship, to apply the name 'God' to anything that is less than God:

'You shall not misuse the name of the Lord your God, for the Lord will not hold anyone guiltless who misuses his name' (Exodus 20:7).

In total, out of ten commandments, the first three are about God and the rejection of all other gods. The heavy emphasis on idolatry makes two things clear: God is Lord over his creation and emphatically not equivalent to it; and those who worship him must become like Abraham. They must leave behind their old world, their old security in old gods of any kind, and enter into an exclusive relationship with Yahweh.

Faithful Love

You have probably noticed that the relationship which the commandments require is like a marriage. In fact, marriage is a recurring image used throughout Hebrew and Christian scripture to capture the essence of Yahweh's relationship to his people. It is exclusive, with no room for other gods.

That God is intent on an intimate relationship with his people brings us to God's love, his most fundamental characteristic. In the Hebrew Bible, God actually stood with Moses and revealed himself, proclaiming:

> 'The Lord, the Lord, the compassionate and gracious
> God, slow to anger, abounding in love and faithfulness,
> maintaining love to thousands, and forgiving wickedness,
> rebellion and sin. Yet he does not leave the guilty
> unpunished; he punishes the children and their children
> for the sin of the fathers to the third and fourth generation'
> (Exodus 34:6–7).

In the New Testament, John puts it with a vast simplicity: 'God is love' (1 John 4:16). Finally, the Qur'an states, 'And He is the Forgiving and Loving' (Qur'an 85:14).[12] Of course, the Jew, Christian and Muslim each claim fundamental differences in their conceptions of God's character, differences that make each of these religions irreducible to any other. Nevertheless, as their starting point, all claim Abraham as their father and his God as their God, the God who is love.

But all three faiths are also clear that love is expressed in action. And this brings us to two of the most fundamental concerns of all religions, including the three monotheistic faiths. How does each religion reconcile its idea of the Divine (or the Ultimate) with a world full of suffering? And, faced with the world's agony, is compassion a sufficient power for dealing with it?

Suffering and Nontheisms

As we have seen, the Hindu idea of the meaning of suffering is tied to the greater order of the universe, a vast harmony in which all things and persons must find and fulfil their place. Each person finds it as she lives rightly, passing through many lifetimes and, because of the law of just consequences (karma), eventually escaping the cycle of rebirth and ascending to blissful union with Brahman, the Ultimate.

In Hinduism, to suffer is to be captive in the world of illusion. In that world, one's specific sufferings result from bad karma, the consequence that one must bear as one learns to live rightly, creating good karma and, ultimately, one's release from illusion.

Buddhism seeks the same release from the created, illusory world. When the young Siddhartha, who later became the Buddha, saw the horrors of disease, crippling age and death, he realized that suffering was the fundamental problem of humanity. He preached that the root of suffering was desire, so each person must learn to extinguish desire. To do that, one must ultimately extinguish self, the chief illusion. Hindus talk about atman, the soul of each person that is part of Brahman, but Buddhists says there is no self. In fact, at the deepest level of reality, there is no 'other'. Everything is a unity. Therefore, one escapes suffering by escaping the illusion of desire, of self, of 'other'. Complete freedom lies beyond self and even beyond being in the uncreated bliss of Nirvana. So suffering and its cure are at the heart of both Hinduism and Buddhism. In each, the remedy is escape from the false reality of self and the world that generates suffering.

It follows that compassion in action, for each of these faiths, is to help others escape from the illusory world and self. Buddha did exactly that, postponing his entrance into bliss and remaining on earth to teach his message to others. Surely the greatest compassion is to help others escape illusion and the suffering of desire that it creates.

Suffering and Monotheism

But among the monotheistic faiths, the world is understood in a profoundly different way. Judaism and Christianity derive their most basic understanding of reality from Genesis, the first book of both the Hebrew and Christian Bibles, which begins with the story of the created world. The famous first verse declares, 'In the beginning God created the heavens and the earth.' This bare sentence makes plain that 'the beginning' was God's project. He precedes the creation and is the source of every created thing. Moreover, God's creation is good. This brief story – little more than a chapter – says six times that God looked at his creation and pronounced it 'good'. A seventh declaration goes even further, pointing out that '... God saw everything that he had made, and behold, it was *very* good' (Genesis 1:31). Seven times the story calls creation good – and, in Hebrew scripture, seven is a very important number. When persons, places, things and events add up to seven, it indicates their thoroughgoing completeness, their special blessedness, their unique and high worth. So when Genesis makes a sevenfold declaration, it can hardly be more clear. From start to finish, all of creation is good. It is not a treacherous illusion that must be transcended.

In the continuing creation story in chapter two, Genesis also points out that within the good creation is the good creature called Adam (a Hebrew word that means 'humankind'). Even more, humankind is actually made 'in the image of God' (Genesis 1:27), which means many things – humans have a spiritual nature, a moral nature, and are capable of free choice. Most importantly, it means that humans are able to love freely. They have the power to freely choose relationships of love with God and with each other.

In addition to showing the essential core of humanity, the Genesis creation story also describes humanity's purpose very plainly. Adam and Eve are placed in the garden of Eden to care for it. The garden is God's. Humans are God's appointed gardeners. They act on his behalf, empowered to pour out his loving nurture on every created thing.

This is why, in Genesis, humankind's fall from perfect, intimate relationship with God is so disastrous. Not only does humankind cut itself off from God, the source of all life, it also deprives the entire creation of that limitless life. When the caretakers of creation walk away from God, the creation inevitably suffers as well.

The Genesis story makes this clear in several ways. A better understanding of the effects of the fall begins with a fresh look at the only forbidden fruit in Eden. In Genesis, God says that only one fruit is off-limits – the one from the tree of 'the knowledge of good and evil' (2:17). We should understand that the fruit is forbidden not because God is selfish or stingy, since he has already declared openly to Adam and Eve that they may eat of any tree in the garden – even the Tree of Life. Rather, God forbids a single, particular fruit because it is the only one in all creation that is poisonous to humans. Genesis is clear that what destroys humans is 'the knowledge of good and evil'.

Paradise Betrayed

Now, with all this background in mind, note what happens after the first people eat the poisonous fruit. First, and for the first time in human existence, they are utterly ashamed to be seen naked. Second, they are so afraid of God that they try to hide from him. This is futile, of course – who can hide from God? – but it shows how they are already losing touch with reality. Third, when God finds them and questions them, each blames the other for ruining their harmony with God. Fourth, God tells them that the ruined harmony is far greater than they imaged. Now all of human experience – living on earth, creating new generations and living with each other – will be a struggle against constant discord. Where it used to be overflowing with life itself, life on earth will now be a constant battle against death.

This is how Genesis describes reality – the reality of God, of creation, of humanity and of humanity's basic conflict. This description is fundamentally different from the non-monotheistic view.

Monotheism is Not Monolithic

However, while all monotheistic religions find their God in the Genesis story of Abraham, they disagree about the Genesis story of creation. Islam sees the world as Allah's creation and no illusion, but it is less concerned with the goodness of creation, humanity's role as its caretaker and the human dilemma. Genesis goes to great lengths to show the interconnection of God, humanity and the rest of the creation, an interconnection so intimate that Adam and Eve's mistrust of God brings the effects of death to all creation. In Islam, though, the connections between Allah, humanity and the world are far more distant, so that the consequences of sin are more limited and more easily remedied. Accordingly, when a Muslim disobeys Allah, the disaster is much more a matter between that person and Allah. When the man confesses and repents, Allah bestows forgiveness. In Islam, humankind is fully able to recognize its sin and fully able to improve. Allah does not require sacrifices for sin and certainly does not sacrifice himself for the sins of others. He speaks the word and forgiveness is complete. Overall, Islam emphasizes that the created world is primarily a realm of testing meant to reveal one's devotion to Allah and, accordingly, one's ultimate fate in paradise or hell. The idea that the world is an obstacle course on the way to heaven bears a certain similarity to the nontheistic religions' view of the world as a maze of illusions that must be escaped in order to reach Brahman or Nirvana.

To sum up, the deep problem of God and suffering is addressed by all the world's great religions, but they answer it in very different ways. Hinduism and Buddhism see human suffering as the result of human entanglement with illusion and desire. In contrast, monotheistic religions see suffering as the result of humanity's freely chosen mistrust of a good God. Judaism and Christianity agree that humankind's fall was a disaster for the entire creation, while Islam gives the problem less emphasis.

God the Rescuer
Judaism says that God himself comes to rescue humanity. God's rescue plan unfolds in history, not just in human imagination or through philosophical insight. Deliverance comes through God's agreement with Israel. If they consent to trust him, he will shape them into his new humanity who will do what Adam and Eve failed to do. Israel will serve all humanity and mediate the saving goodness of God to the whole world.

Today, in at least part of Jewish understanding, God's chosen people are still appointed to play their role as God's servant for the world. But another tradition holds that the most important part of Israel's service to the world is to bring forth the messiah, a Hebrew term that means 'anointed one'. As the Hebrew scriptures foretell, the messiah is anointed to be the final king, the bringer of perfect justice for Israel and the whole world. When he comes, he will usher in God's endless kingdom and the final rule of God for everyone everywhere. Jews who believe in the coming messiah still wait for him to appear.

It was the wait for the messiah that formed the foundation of Christianity. Beginning in roughly 30 CE, a group of Jews in Palestine became convinced that the wait had suddenly ended and the messiah had actually arrived in Jesus of Nazareth. His ringing message of repentance and forgiveness truly echoed the Hebrew prophets. The crowds that followed Jesus swelled as the news spread of his miracles of healing the sick, feeding the hungry, freeing the demon-bound and even raising the dead. But a smaller following recognized the greater meaning – that Jesus' acts were those that scripture predicted the messiah would perform. These disciples became convinced he would usher in the kingdom of God and, especially, Israel's deliverance from oppression.

Messiah the Victim

But instead of setting up a new kingdom, Jesus became one more victim of the current kingdom. Seen as a threat to the status quo, Jesus was convicted of the capital crime of blasphemy, and the sentence was carried out courtesy of the despised Roman occupiers, who reserved to themselves the power of execution. The Jesus movement, like other supposed messianic outbreaks before it, was extinguished with its leader.

But of course the Jesus movement was only starting. Within days of his crucifixion, eyewitnesses were spreading the staggering message that Jesus was alive again. In a great reversal, he had, by his resurrection, conquered evil and death – and every power of their making – through the 'weakness' of unarmed love. Jesus was indeed the messiah, and a far greater one than his followers ever imagined. He was, like God, Lord of all.

And here is the strangest answer to suffering found among any of the major religions. Like Jews, Christians understand suffering to be real and not illusory, the result of mankind's desertion of God. But Christians say that, in the person of Jesus Christ, it is God himself who bears all the degrading consequences of evil. For the humans who betrayed him, God dies their death and gives them his life.

Love That Suffers

Consequently, Christians' approach to suffering is to love as they have been loved. Compassion leads them to enter into the suffering of others, relieving it when possible but sharing it always, even giving their lives for the lives of others. Of course, many Christians famously fail to fulfil this high calling. Less famously, many succeed.

The Christian understanding of suffering and compassion is inherited directly from Judaism – Jesus continually cited the Hebrew scriptures as the confirmation of his teaching. Of course, Judaism does not believe that Jesus is the Jewish messiah, so it does not view his personal suffering as an effective cure for evil. Instead, Judaism sees the proof of God's complete commitment to justice and mercy in his loyal, loving relationship with his people. The Hebrew Bible brims with God's command to seek justice and mercy on behalf of every member of society, especially the weak and the poor, and even the 'foreigners' and 'sojourners' in their midst. In modern language, by the way, 'foreigners' means immigrants and resident aliens and 'sojourners' means those who are resident temporarily on their journey elsewhere.

Islam also rejects the idea of Jesus as a suffering, divine saviour, but for different reasons. First, the idea of a suffering God is impossibly unjust – Allah has never done the slightest evil and can never deserve its consequences. Second, a suffering God is a blasphemy. It is far beneath Allah's majesty that he should be like humans at all, let alone in their weakness. To equate man or anything else with Allah is the grave sin known as 'shirk', a word that translates as 'association' and 'polytheism'. Of course, to assert that the man Jesus is part of God's person is shirk of the most extreme sort.

Yet Islam holds Jesus in high honour as the prophet second only to Muhammad. And because Allah is just, he could never permit the gross injustice of a prophet's crucifixion. Therefore, it cannot be that Jesus actually died on a Roman cross. Instead, Muslims believe, his crucifixion and resurrection is a falsehood perpetrated by Christians – a deception that persists to this day, passed down through gross errors and deliberate lies inserted in the badly transmitted texts of the New Testament.

Compassion Proves Itself

As you can see, the great religions all understand suffering in different ways. To simplify all these views of suffering and compassion, it might be useful to consider Jesus' well-known story of the Good Samaritan. In it Jesus tells of a Jewish traveller who is attacked on the road by thieves who savagely beat him, strip him of every last item – even his clothing – and leave him for dead. To make the point that a man's commitment to do what God commands and 'love your neighbour as yourself' (Leviticus 19:18) is shown not by words but by deeds, Jesus continues his story by telling of a very religious traveller who completely ignores the victim on the road, followed by a second, equally religious traveller who does the same. The only traveller who does what is right is a 'Samaritan' – a man whose ethnic heritage marked him for Jesus' listeners as a traitor and hereditary enemy. The Samaritan shows mercy to the robbers' victim, risking his own safety, pouring out his time and money and upsetting his own business plans to give the man the full care that he, the Samaritan, would want for himself – and could never expect from other travellers if he were the victim on the road.

Now imagine the dying victim on the road approached by modern people of the five great religions. A Hindu might be within his rights to withhold himself from the suffering victim to avoid entanglement in the illusion of need and desire. Perhaps a Buddhist could do likewise for the same reason. He could even note to himself that the young Siddhartha, encountering suffering for the first time, only observed it and did not relieve it. Or perhaps a Jew, like those Jews in the original parable, would retreat into legalism about the ritual uncleanness that comes from touching (what might be) a dead body. Maybe a Christian would tell himself he had no time to stop because crucial religious work waited for him in the next town. Certainly a Muslim might reason that, though he would be duty-bound to help a Muslim victim, nursing a probable infidel like this man was another matter.

Beyond Religion as Usual

According to Jesus, all of them would be wrong. His starting point is the authoritative command to 'love your neighbour as yourself', but his parable changes the conventional interpretation in two important ways. First, it simply puts a stop to every attempt to say that 'neighbours' does not include 'foreigners', the former who must be loved and the latter who may be ignored. In Jesus' story, 'neighbour' is the only category. It applies to every person, including the next person you find on the road. But there is more. Jesus' simple story shifts the moral scrutiny from grading 'neighbours' to grading oneself. The question is no longer 'Who is my neighbour?' Unexpectedly, it has become 'Am I a neighbour? Will I show mercy to the next person I encounter?'

This question is near to the heart of Jewish monotheism, in which God continually commands his people to 'love your neighbour as yourself'. Jesus moves this command into the centre. He equates it with the highest law in Judaism – 'Love the Lord your God with all your heart and with all your soul and with all your strength' (Deuteronomy 6:5) – and declares that the love of God and the love of neighbour are the inseparable heart of God's law.

All great religions contemplate deeply why we suffer. None asks the question quite the same way and none offers quite the same answer. None answers it completely. But for a refuge from suffering, each religion turns to its best understanding of compassion.

CHAPTER 6

God in the Scriptures of Monotheism

Judaism, Christianity and Islam are monotheistic faiths that each proclaim the one God.

But their disagreements about this God go deep, down to the bedrock of their respective scriptures – the Hebrew Bible, the Christian Bible, and the Qur'an. It is time to look more closely at what each text says about God.

The Hebrew Bible

The Hebrew Bible is the most ancient of the three. It is a richly varied library of writings gathered over centuries and put in its final form by around 100 CE. The word 'bible' comes from the Latin word '*biblia*' and simply means 'books', which are abundant in the Hebrew Bible – books of history, stories, law code, poetry, songs, prophecy and more. Yet remarkably, through all these kinds of literature, written so many centuries apart, there run consistent themes that reveal a profound and unique understanding of God. The Hebrew Bible is also recognized by Christians as scripture and appears in their Bible as the Old Testament. More on this later.

In the Beginning, God

Look again at the Hebrew Bible's first verse: 'In the beginning, God created the heavens and the earth' (Genesis 1:1). When the ancient Hebrews first made this radical proclamation of one Lord of all, they lived in a world filled everywhere with gods. Surrounding the Jews were cultures with their own creation stories in which the powerful local god made earth and sky – but was himself subject to the fundamental blind fate behind all things. The great Babylonian god Marduk, for example, formed heaven and earth, but only after his own origination out of the primal chaos.

In the midst of all these cultures the ancient Hebrews said something entirely new, something so radically different that it set them apart from all the peoples of the earth. They declared that, before any beginning, there was God – the only source, preceded by nothing, God alone. This idea of one God and only one God is the Hebrew Bible's first and most fundamental declaration about God's character.

God Loves

But this first unique declaration in Genesis is the foundation for another of even greater impact: though God is the one above all, he is also a God of intimate relationship. This picture, which stands in utter contrast to the gods of surrounding cultures, is expressed powerfully once again in Genesis. In its creation stories, God makes man 'in his own image'. These four bare words describe the staggering endowment granted to nothing else in all creation. As noted in the previous chapter, this immeasurable gift bestows the power of free will, creativity and reason, but most of all, humanity receives the power to live, like God, in the closest relationships of love. The text is bold to explain just how intimate that love can be: 'So God created man in his own image, in the image of God he created him; *male and female he created them*' (Genesis 1:27). The implication is that God enjoys a mysterious and deep communion within himself, and that, because they bear his image, men and women can share a similarly profound love with him and with each other.

This powerful portrayal of people in personal relationship to God is far different from what was found in pagan cultures of the time, whose nature gods were rooted in specific geographic areas. A people's god depended on their locale rather than on intentional relationship. Moreover, though the people were beholden to their local gods for rains and crops, the gods were also dependent on their people. The gods grew weak. They required their worshippers to strengthen and nourish them by means of the proper rituals and by sacrifices of food. Even ritual prostitution was necessary so that the watching sky god would be sufficiently excited to fertilize the earth goddess with the rains that brought fruitful harvests. The gods and the people were dependent on each other, but it was not love. At bottom, it was magic and the Hebrew Bible rejected it.

God Redeems

Of course, truly intimate relationships cannot exist without true freedom – and true freedom possesses the terrible power to betray. In the Genesis creation stories, the first humans have that awful freedom and, in the end, they use it to abandon God for a serpent's lie about a better future. When they betray their intimate friendship with God, the result is shame, fear, conflict and death. But God does not abandon his humans. He comes to them, speaks with them and equips them for the uncertain life ahead. And here the Hebrew Bible begins to reveal a third great characteristic of God: from the beginning of the scripture to the end, God is the redeemer.

The story of the God who redeems begins in Genesis with the first humans, Adam and Eve, but unfolds fully in the Hebrew Bible's great central epic of the relationship between God and Israel. This account takes place not in a legend or an ode but in the concrete world of human history, in a definite time and place and, most importantly, among a particular people.

In the Hebrew Bible, God chooses Israel for an intimate relationship with him. Today's readers may object that God is playing favourites, but nowhere does the account contain the slightest hint that God has chosen Israel for any virtue of its own. In fact, the Hebrew Bible supplies a full record of Israel's continuing misdeeds. Instead, it becomes clear that God has chosen Israel for the sake of all mankind. In Israel, the world is supposed to see what God is really like. Here the nations may see that the people who know and love the one God live in justice, mercy and peace and that God, ultimately, will extend his blessings through Israel to all of humanity.

That, at least, is the plan. What actually happens is a long and harrowing reprise of the trouble in Eden. But through all of Israel's history, whether Israel clings to God or drifts far from him, God holds them fast and, in the end, redeems them from evil.

Grace in History

As we have seen, the great history of Israel's call begins with Abram, a city dweller who practises the traditional polytheism of his people. Then the one God encounters him, telling Abram to leave his homeland and the gods of his ancestors and go into an unknown future in 'the land I will show you' (Genesis 12:1). Abram agrees and obeys – and so begins the long history of God, Israel and the nations.

The foundation of that long history is simply God's grace. He chooses to bless Israel, to be faithful to them, and, even when they wander from him, to redeem them and bring them back.

This unique theme of redeeming love runs through the entire story of Israel – their emergence as a people, their enslavement in Egypt, their miraculous deliverance from slavery, their establishment in the land of promise, the rise and fall of their kingdoms, the cries of their prophets to return to God and their prophets' strong and comforting assurances that God will keep his side of the covenant to the end.

God Delivers Israel

Nowhere in the Hebrew Bible does God's redeeming character come through more strongly than in the story of the exodus – God's deliverance of Israel from bondage in Egypt, the superpower of its time. No force on earth could make them relinquish their slaves, but in the one God, Egypt encountered a deliverer of inconceivable strength. Through his emissary, Moses, God warns Pharaoh, the Egyptian king, to free Israel, but Pharaoh refuses – and thereby brings down God's destruction on his nation and, most of all, his nation's gods. The waters of the Nile, life-giving gift of Hapi, the father of the gods, are turned to blood. Frogs, sacred to the gods Heka and Osiris, are made to swarm, die, rot and defile the land. Plague after plague brings devastating proof that nothing, not even Egypt's gods, can protect the Egyptians from the one God, the God who has bound himself to Israel.

But despite the futility of warring against God, Pharaoh still defies him – and thereby sets in motion the most fearsome sentence of all. Pharaoh was considered a god who, in time, would be succeeded by a divine heir in the person of Pharaoh's first-born son. Against these supposed gods, the one God at last sends the enemy no one can withstand – the death angel. Passing through the entire land, the death angel will touch every first-born, even among the animals. Not one of Egypt's households will have the power to save itself from the coming stroke of death.

But God, Israel's redeemer, will protect his people. And he will do it through the blood of a lamb. God tells the people that each household must kill an unblemished lamb and paint its blood on their doorposts. When the death angel sees the blood, he will not enter. He will pass over.

Later, when the angel's onslaught is ended, the people of Egypt have lost not only their first-born, but their entire divine order as well. Pharaoh's first-born son, the future god-king, is dead. But God's people have been shielded from destruction by the symbolic death of the sacrificial lamb. Pharaoh cries out and commands

Israel to leave at once. Saved from death, Israel leaves the land of slavery and journeys to the land of promise.

Atoning Sacrifice

As their new life in freedom develops, Israel institutes a system of ritual sacrifice as part of its national pattern of worship. And though the surrounding nations also have sacrificial systems, the meaning of Israel's sacrifices is strikingly different. The nearby nations sacrifice to feed their gods, to prod them into action and to assuage their displeasure. But the Jewish system provides sacrifices that hearken back to the Passover lamb, the sacrifice that shielded the people from death. In Israel, a pure life, symbolized by a ritually clean animal, may suffer death to atone for the worshipper. The sacrificial system is detailed in the Hebrew Bible's book of Leviticus, a record of law.

To sum up, the Hebrew Bible says three stunning things about God: God is one; God is relational; and when that relationship is broken, God redeems.

The Christian Bible

How, then, is God characterized in the Christian Bible? In great measure, the Christian God is identical to the God of the Hebrew Bible. After all, the Hebrew Bible itself constitutes the largest section of the Christian Bible, where it is renamed the 'Old Testament'.

But the Christian Bible also contains a second section called the New Testament, which contains, Christians say, the authoritative account of God's most important breakthrough into the world – an invasion that reveals to the whole world the full expression of God's character. This pivotal event took place after the Old Testament was complete, so only together can the Old and New Testaments tell the full story of God's redemption of his people. For its part, the Old Testament is indispensable for two reasons. First, it records the sweep of God's great redeeming purpose, especially in his historical relationship with the people of Israel. Second, it foresees the coming of the messiah, the divinely anointed king who will one day reign over Israel in a future golden age. In the New Testament, the miracle has happened – the coming messiah has been revealed, has defeated his foes, and has begun his triumphant, eternal rule. Who he is, what he accomplished, what it all means and what is to come – this is the entire focus of the New Testament.

The Unlikely Messiah

In order to see the character of God as revealed in his messiah, it is necessary to know the messiah's story, which the New Testament tells in its four Gospel accounts (the word 'gospel' means 'good news'). Here God's anointed launches his rule like no king the world would recognize. He is born in Palestine, a distant, conquered province of the Roman empire. After a thinly reported youth and an entirely obscure career as a carpenter, he begins his work. The year is around 30 CE.

Poor and on foot, Jesus of Nazareth travels the countryside teaching and ministering to the commoners, but he speaks and acts with striking power and authority. It is as though he were speaking and acting on behalf of God himself. Jesus brings hope to the hopeless, relief to the suffering, food to the hungry, freedom to the oppressed and judgment to the powers that be. His disciples see his works, hear his words, ponder the scriptures of the Hebrew Bible and come to believe that Jesus is indeed the predicted messiah, the one who will lead Israel into a golden age of redemption.

Death and the End of Death

Throughout the region, Jesus declares that 'the kingdom of God' has appeared and that anyone, high or low, may enter by turning again to God and by believing in 'the one he has sent' (John 6:29) – the one who will also 'give his life as a ransom for many' (Matthew 20:28). In three short years, his message and his person cause a tumult. Many believe he is sent from God, though some say he is of the Devil. In the end, the Jewish and Roman authorities work together to condemn Jesus for blasphemy and sedition. His death is by crucifixion – the torture-execution method used by the Romans to destroy and degrade slaves, rebels and other especially despised criminals.

His death cuts off any possibility that he was the messiah. It is hopeless to imagine that he might have delivered Israel from captivity. The Jesus movement is ready to die like its leader.

But the impossible news comes to his disciples that Jesus has risen from death. Initially they disbelieve, but in a short while they encounter Jesus again, face to face. He appears among them, walks with them, speaks with them and even eats with them. Over the following weeks, he tells them to proclaim the news of his redeeming victory to the whole world. Finally, he departs from them into heaven, speaking his final words: 'And surely I am with you always, to the very end of the age' (Matthew 28:20).

The Whole Creation Renewed

This is the account of God's messiah as told in the Gospels of the New Testament. In them and its other writings, the New Testament further explains what this transforming event means. It declares that Jesus is a far greater messiah than ever imagined. In fact, the writers say that it is God himself who has come, literally in the flesh, in the person of Jesus. His ministry has offered a preview of God's kingdom, summed up in a famous verse which reports that '… the blind receive sight, the lame walk, those who have leprosy are cured, the deaf hear, the dead are raised, and the good news is preached to the poor' (Luke 7:22). This list directly invokes the words of the Old Testament's great prophet Isaiah when he describes the coming, joyful deliverance of Israel.

Furthermore, the New Testament is bold to proclaim that, through his messiah, Jesus, God's love and redemption now reaches to everyone. As God delivered Israel out of slavery in Egypt, he has now delivered all humanity from its enslavement to evil, sin and death. As the blood of a sacrificial lamb shielded the Israelites from death during the exodus, God has now provided the ultimate sacrificial lamb in the God–man Jesus Christ, whose death has ended the power of death forever. As God brought Israel into the promised land, he has now offered citizenship in his kingdom to all humanity, a citizenship that begins now and goes on forever in the age to come.

This is the New Testament's message of God's love and Christ's redemption. Here is God's awesome 'new covenant' with mankind, God's pledge of faithful love and redemption that expands his older covenant with Israel. Note that another word for 'covenant' is 'testament'. In the Old Testament and the New Testament, Christians find the complete story of God's loving purposes.

From this quick overview of the New Testament's story, the Christian understanding of God's character emerges. Everything of the Jewish picture is here – God's oneness, God's deeply relational character, God's redemptive heart – but the New Testament adds to them the person of Jesus, God's messiah, who has achieved universal redemption for all.

Three in One, One in Three

Because of its message of Jesus, the New Testament ultimately characterizes God in a shocking new way. On the one hand, it insists on the traditional Jewish understanding that God is one. But on the other hand, it talks about Jesus and the Holy Spirit as if they also are God. What can this mean? How can God be one and also be three? From this paradox emerged the doctrine of the Trinity, which delves deeply into the Christian Bible, as well as language, theology and philosophy, to explain that God is three individual realities united in one entity. He is an interrelationship of love – interconnected, united and necessary – somewhat like the lover, the beloved and the love. He is three forms of one person, like the speaker, the spoken word and the breath. In the end, though, the analogies and the theologies all fall short. And still the New Testament alludes to a triune God who is one.

As you can imagine, the Christian characterization of God hardly brings approving nods from the monotheistic Jews and Muslims. For Jews, the Trinity is an impossible by-product of the Christian view of Jesus – a view that comes, in part, from wrongly interpreting the Hebrew Bible. In fact, the Christian conclusion that Jesus is the Hebrew Bible's messiah assails the foundations of Jewish belief. Maybe that is why Jews and Christians can argue endlessly about the meaning of the Hebrew scripture. But no matter how they might argue, it is essential to understand that, though Jews and Christians disagree deeply about the interpretation of the Hebrew Bible, they do not much argue about its textual content – its words and sentences. They agree that they are reading the same book.

Muslims see it very differently. They also reject any talk of a Trinity, but go much further than simply arguing about interpretation. They accept neither the Hebrew nor Christian Bibles as they stand in Judaism and Christianity.

The Qur'an
This brings us to God as he is revealed in the Qur'an, the scripture of the world's third great monotheistic religion. The Qur'an's central message is phrased most powerfully and simply in a sort of creedal statement cherished by Muslims worldwide and known as the Five Pillars of Faith. The first of the Pillars, called the Shahadah, declares, 'There is no God but Allah and Muhammad is his prophet.'

The Shahadah states simply what the Qur'an declares everywhere from beginning to end – Allah is the one God, the only God, and no one and nothing is like him. Even Muhammad, though he is the last and greatest prophet and the exemplary man, is a man only. Allah stands alone, above all and over all, without peer and without comparison. In fact, his name, Al-Lah, means literally 'The God'. Accordingly, as the Qur'an makes clear, the greatest sin is to suggest that anyone or anything can share, however slightly, in the divine transcendence of Allah.

Allah the Compassionate

The Qur'an is a brief book, about as long as the New Testament, and it is divided into 114 chapters, some as brief as a few sentences. Each chapter is called a 'sura', and no matter what its length, every sura but one begins with this: 'In the name of God, the Compassionate, the Merciful'. God's love, therefore, stands as a constant introduction to everything the Qur'an has to say.

The love of Allah is above all practical. He insists on fairness to all and mercy towards the needy. He forgives the repentant and exhorts them to produce the righteous acts that prove their repentance. He rewards those on the straight path of true submission to God. He dooms those who habitually refuse the clear call of submission to his sovereignty.

Even though Allah is inconceivably beyond humankind, he wants to be known. And he can be when one reads the signs. These signs are all around us – in nature and, with purest clarity, in the Qur'an. To hear the Qur'an is to hear the very words of God, the complete, abundant and final sign. Especially beloved are the signs contained in the Ninety-nine Beautiful Names of God, a litany of the most prized among all of Allah's abundant attributes found in the Qur'an. His names include al-Awwal, the First; al-Akhir, the Last; al-Badi', the Maker; al-Barr, the Beneficent; al-Basir, the Observant; al-Batin, the Inner; al-Tawwab, the Relenting; al-Hassib, the Accounter; al-Haqq, the Truth; and dozens more which, together, reveal the vast and awesome Lord.

God Alone

So far, the God of the Qur'an seems very much like the God of the Hebrew and Christian Bibles. Those two scriptures declare that God is one God, a statement with which the Qur'an agrees emphatically. But from this point forward, the differences begin to grow.

First, the Qur'an puts strong emphasis on Allah's exalted transcendence. Because he is almighty in power, righteousness and truth, humans will find peace and joy only in complete submission to his will. Submission is the heart of Islam. In fact, the Arabic word for 'submission' contains the same Arabic root ('s-l-m') that appears in four other Arabic words – words that mean 'peace', 'safety', 'Islam' and 'Muslim'. Peace and harmony come from realizing the towering greatness of Allah and wholly accepting his rule.

By contrast, the Hebrew Bible describes the Jewish God in terms too earthly for the Qur'an. Yahweh weeps, flares in anger and rejoices over his people. He is personal and immediate. But Allah is greater, high above all – including metaphors that might describe him in too-human terms.

The Qur'an Corrects the Bible

Because Allah is God over all, it follows that his actual words, which are recorded in the Qur'an, must stand above every other revelation. Though the Hebrew and Christian Bibles precede it by centuries, the Qur'an is the foundation of all truth, past, present and future. The Qur'an is the full and final revelation of God to mankind.

Furthermore, the Qur'an says that the problem with the scriptures of the Jews and Christians is more than a problem of interpretation. The Hebrew and Christian Bibles require basic changes to the texts themselves. The meaning of each Bible is wrong because, in essential texts, the words themselves are wrong. For many of those errors, the Qur'an provides correction and explanation.

Even so, there is truth in the Hebrew and Christian Bibles. Any reader may find it by simply comparing those books to the Qur'an. Where they follow the Qur'an, the Qur'an itself declares them valid revelations sent from Allah. But where they depart from the Qur'an, the Bibles are grievously errant – not because Allah did not grant a clear revelation in the past, but because his clear revelation has been obscured over the centuries by a great accretion of wayward mistakes and intentional misrepresentations. Unblemished revelation comes from the Qur'an, which is God's absolute truth, free of all errors.

In addition to rejecting actual texts of the Hebrew and Christian Bibles, the Qur'an also rejects some of their most basic themes. For instance, the Qur'an rejects their view of human nature. It is wrong to say that man is made 'in the image' of God. Not only is Allah far too exalted for this, but the whole idea suggests that man shares in God's person, which is blasphemous 'shirk'.

But the Qur'an does endow each person with God's divine spark in the form of 'taqwa'. Taqwa is the inner awareness of God, of one's relationship and responsibility to him, that reveals itself in one's conscience. To be fully human, every person must cultivate conscience, listening to its call for submission to Allah. Listening or not, submitting or not, these are up to each person.

Moreover, each person has the power to choose. The Qur'an rejects the biblical idea that humanity is powerless to restore itself to God. Instead, people are born perfect and can choose freely between good and evil, so when a man sins, he sins by his own unfettered choice. Having chosen evil, he will receive the fair, reasonable and terrible punishment of Allah at the judgment. But because he is completely free to choose good or evil, a man can also repent. He can admit his evil choices, ask forgiveness of Allah, submit to him and begin doing those deeds that prove his change of heart. If he remains on the straight path, Allah will reward him. But in the end, whether Allah punishes or rewards will depend on what a person chooses.

Forgiveness

In the Qur'an, Allah needs no system of atonement to forgive a man his sin. Allah speaks the word, if he will, and the man is forgiven. In fact, sacrifice and atonement can even be seen as 'shirk', since they suggest that a system or creature may somehow be required to transmit or aid the forgiving power of Allah.

It is no surprise, then, that the Qur'an completely rejects the son of God described in the New Testament. Jesus cannot be God's son, since any such relationship could only be 'shirk'. His resurrection as Lord of all is blasphemy.

Yet the Qur'an declares Jesus a great prophet of Allah, despite the New Testament texts that speak of Jesus' divinity. The Qur'an simply rejects them, using its own authoritative revelations about Jesus to correct the Christian scripture. For example, the Qur'an records a conversation that the New Testament does not, in which Allah speaks with Jesus. Allah asks if Jesus ever told people to regard Jesus as divine. Jesus heartily denies it. The Qur'an also declares that Jesus was definitely not crucified, for how could God's prophet be so unjustly destroyed? What the New Testament texts fail to report is that Jesus was delivered by Allah from his enemies, who were left deceived and merely presuming they had killed Jesus.

So in some ways the God of the Qur'an is like the Hebrew and Christian God, but he also stands well apart. Allah is the only God; Allah reveals himself, fully and finally, by speaking the Qur'an; Allah is righteous and will reward and punish fairly on the day of judgment.

One God?

In the end, the three great monotheistic faiths agree that God is one. But they disagree on the character of that God and even on what is meant by oneness. And each stands firm on the authority of its own revealed scripture. By any measure, they have plenty of non-negotiable differences.

But remarkably, they share the clear commands to act in complete fairness, be merciful to the poor and the needy and be humble before God. If the followers of these three global faiths could agree to actually live out these common commands, then perhaps they could live fairly, mercifully and humbly not only with God but also with each other.

CHAPTER 7

Desire for God vs Desire for God's Power

True religion, as defined by the Hebrew Bible and affirmed by Jesus, is to love God utterly and to love your neighbour as fully as you love yourself.

Magic, by comparison, has a very different interest in God and neighbour. Ultimately, it views them as useful sources of power, for sorcerers want to control both the natural and supernatural worlds for their own ends. In our scientific age, we no longer believe in magic, but we certainly believe in its purpose. The urge to control is ever with us, often as a means to good ends and always as a temptation to evil.

The desire for God and the desire for God's power – these are in constant opposition within us. And the line between them is always blurry for the simple reason that human motives are blurry. On the one hand, we want to worship the Almighty. On the other hand, we want to *be* the Almighty. The great monotheistic religions call us to God and his kingdom, but something within whispers that there is an even better world, a shining kingdom in which we, not God, possess the power. Call that whisper the magical temptation.

We can see it at work in the nature religions of the ancient world. Certainly the powers of nature called forth the impulse to simply worship their sheer magnificence. However, worshippers also worked to manipulate the supernatural powers with rituals that would cause them to yield rain, sun and health and divert storm, sickness and war.

Beyond these not unreasonable purposes, however, the magical temptation suggested that the powers could be harnessed for even greater possibilities. Why not use them to afflict your communal enemies? How about your personal enemies as well? And what about personal wealth and influence? In fact, why not harness god-power for complete personal power? Why not switch places with the gods – you command and they obey? This is the fundamental question that the magical temptation raises. And the implied answer is always the same – it is better to be a god than a god's servant.

Nature religions and magic thrived everywhere and the Ancient Near East was no exception. Among the Jews, however, monotheism stood in sharp contrast, declaring that the God of Israel was not just another nature god, but God alone and, even more, the ultimate person, who seeks loving relationship with humankind.

Perhaps that is why the Jewish story of creation in Genesis shows Adam and Eve tempted by the old magical proposition. The serpent explains it: eating the apple will not bring death (inferring, incidentally, that the apple is not dangerous and God is a liar), but will instead open a new life of limitless control. 'You will be like God,' it says, 'knowing good and evil' (Genesis 3:5). Scholars say that the phrase 'good and evil' is probably a literary device called a 'merism', in which two items are the bookends on either end of a complete range. We use this device every day in expressions such as 'everything from A to Z' and 'searched high and low'. So the serpent's offer is the ultimate temptation – eat the fruit that God has warned against, fruit from the Tree of Complete Knowledge, and you will be like God, filled with limitless knowing and the divine life that (allegedly) goes with it.

But the devil is in the details. Just as eating the fruit does not result in instant death, neither does it produce instant knowledge. Instead, knowledge will come over time, step by step. And Adam and Eve's first step into complete knowledge is terrible. They see themselves as they truly are – utterly naked – and they are plunged into deep, inescapable shame.

Driven by their new knowledge and new fear, their first action is, paradoxically, stunningly ignorant. They try to hide from God. Of all the responses they could have chosen, this is the most blind. This impossibility would have been inconceivable in their prior unfallen state. They have gained forbidden knowledge, but it has unreported side effects. It drowns humans in raw ignorance.

The good news in Genesis, of course, is that the wholly good God goes looking for his guilty friends. He finds them and equips them for the coming sorrows of life in the brave new world they have chosen. He first tells them that they will suffer – in work, in childbirth and in their relationships. Then God relieves their shame by clothing them in animal skins. With these skins, death appears for the first time. Perhaps Adam and Eve were shocked to realize that, from now on, they would live because other creatures died. This may be the Bible's first hint about the meaning and importance of sacrifice. Finally, the human pair become refugees driven from Eden.

The story of the fall is humanity's most fundamental lesson about itself. Without it, no one can understand himself, other people or human history. It is the story of each person, in every age, saying 'yes' from the chaotic depths of even the purest heart, to the temptation to be like God. According to Genesis, this is the root of suffering.

But in clear contrast to nontheistic religions, Genesis portrays suffering not as a result of the ego itself and its desires, but as a symptom of something deeper still – the break in our living relationship with the God of life. Genesis suggests that, even if humanity quelled all its suffering, it still could not heal its deepest wound. Somehow humankind must be released from its addiction and enslavement to the magical temptation. But having failed to make itself like God, mankind is also powerless to restore itself to a living relationship with God. The whole of the Bible, however, is the story of God undertaking to restore mankind and the whole creation to himself.

Now, if it were easy, the Bible might be a shorter book. But working in history means working in time, so the account of God's salvation takes time, too. Both Jewish and Christian readers of the Bible agree that God's work in history is still under way, that the happy ending is coming, but no one can say when it will be.

Four Magical Temptations

In the meantime, there are decisions to be made and work to do. And daily, we face the old magical temptation. Even in the search for God – perhaps especially in the search for God – we will soon encounter the subtle invitation to take control and make ourselves the central purpose of everything. Several variations of that temptation are worth examining more closely.

Temptation 1: False Unity

First, consider the idea that 'all religions are basically the same'. At its best, this idea hopes to find in all religions a common core that will end religious divisions and unite all people in a good and true common conviction. The common core most often identified is compassion towards others.

The difficulty, though, is that almost every religion holds that compassion towards others is a side-product of its exclusive central teaching and not an end in itself. In Buddhism, love of neighbour comes along the way to 'no self' and the ultimate realization of Nirvana. Christianity says that deep love of neighbour arises in us when we see and accept the deep, sacrificial love of God for us in Jesus Christ. Islam points to care for our neighbours as an act of obedient submission to the exalted glory and power of Allah.

None of these religions says that its unique content is optional, as long as one shows compassion. The love of neighbour is a product of the religion and not vice versa.

Some may still assert that all these religions misunderstand themselves and are actually about a single, greater truth. But no one can reasonably suggest that these religions have ever understood themselves this way. In the end, the only way one can claim the unity of all religions is to abandon their own reports of themselves and substitute private versions of one's preference.

Given the unique claims that each religion makes for itself, why do people insist that all religions are essentially the same? It seems a bit like insisting that all mammals are essentially ferrets. This magical temptation to believe in a false unity of all religions will keep us from seeing any religion as it is. In the end, it is far more useful – and far simpler – to understand the differences at the heart of each religion and begin the work of understanding why they are different.

However, the magical temptation of false unity can mislead in more dangerous ways when it suggests that, because all religions are the same, one is not subject to the claims of any of them. From a merely logical standpoint, of course, a follower of a universal religion of this sort should be obedient to *all* religious claims. But the real danger is to one's moral and ethical life. Certainly, by the standards of Judaism and Christianity, only false religion can suggest that a man is dismissed from heeding the prophets' calls to self-examination, repentance and devotion to justice and mercy. And, at minimum, all religions actually do agree on this – a true follower must be a doer of her religion and not just a spectator. Charles Wesley, the eighteenth-century Methodist leader, said something similar: 'An atheist is a person who lives day to day as if God makes no difference.' By this very pragmatic definition, the world is full of unbelievers, both religious and otherwise.

Temptation 2: False Separation

Fundamentalism is a word we use chiefly in discussing religious factions, but fundamentalism comes in all sorts of varieties – political, cultural, even economic, to name a few. No matter what the variation, underlying them all is the same magical temptation to separate from others on the grounds of greater purity. More importantly, this magical temptation suggests that because we are more pure – more correct, more right, more righteous – we are surrounded by the impure. Sooner or later, the impure will constitute a threat to our purity.

Even among those who have separated themselves, the threat of impurity is close at hand. A pure leader rises and, in time, is deposed by one who is purer still. Purges rage, factions split off, and on the far fringes, cults barricade themselves inside their compounds.

It bears repeating that this false separation based on false purity is not a magical temptation of the religious alone. Every breathing human is subject to its false promise which, if left to fester, can have unspeakable results. Witness the mass violence of the politically pure that so plagued the last century, both in Nazi Germany and in Soviet Russia, and that still afflicts Zimbabwe, Malaysia, North Korea, China and their fellow police states.

Temptation 3: False Hope

It was during the Enlightenment of the eighteenth century that Western thinkers, roughly speaking, switched places with God. As the foundation of knowledge, revelation was replaced by human reason. God moved out, becoming the absentee landlord of deism, and humankind moved to the centre of things. When it came to understanding the creation and everything in it, the source of humanity's enlightenment became the rational mind of humanity itself.

From this new perspective, philosophy and natural science made great strides, and, by the end of the nineteenth century, major innovations, such as democracy and germ theory, had produced vast improvements in the lives of millions. Human life was getting better.

Some hoped that what was getting better was humanity itself. Arising shortly after the Enlightenment, the Romantic movement rejected what it saw as the too-rigid rationality of the Enlightenment and looked to humanity's deeper intuitions and feelings for the human progress that would, in the fullness of time, lead to human perfectibility. By the 1850s, the Realist movement was setting itself directly opposite the Romantics and their too-idealized view of humanity.

Even so, many of Romanticism's ideals live on today, particularly in the contemporary movement known as the New Spirituality, drawing as it does on any and every religious, spiritual, mystical and scientific source to cobble together an eclectic vision of humanity and its sure potential for progress.

And here is the point: the idea that humans are getting better and better can easily become a third magical temptation, this time of false hope. Those religions, movements, '-isms' and '-ologies' that promise that humanity will perfect humanity are, bluntly, a waste of time.

The whole of human history is a perfect record of our spiritual failure: not one righteous kingdom, not one perfectly just legal system, not a single just war, not a single pure revolution, not a single untainted economy anywhere in all history. Human failure at self-perfection surely must be history's greatest, most obvious and most important lesson.

This sounds like very bad news indeed. But it is accurate news, an explanation that fits the evidence and brings us to the heart of the matter: maybe our failures are trying to tell us something. They are saying that we fail to achieve perfect love of God and neighbour because such love simply is not in us. We may do good works, but no matter how many we do or how hard we try, the distance between us and pure goodness remains the same.

We must not be distracted by the magical temptation that we can still make ourselves into what we ought to be. If, in all these millennia, a single human has yet to live an untainted life, what new human capacity will change this? If mankind's greatest goal is goodness, why have we not achieved it by now?

Buddhists may object that goodness is not the point, that goodness and compassion will emerge when one sheds the illusion of the self and sees that all is One. But among all enlightened Buddhists, where are the perfectly compassionate, those who love their neighbours as fully as they love themselves? Lay aside all the complications of defining 'self', 'Self' and even 'compassion'. Where is any Buddhist who perfectly loves his neighbour, who has never wronged another? Where is any Hindu who has never put a secret self-interest ahead of his neighbour's need?

This is not to single out the failings of the nontheistic religions. The same is true of every monotheistic faith and, more personally, of every individual Jew, Christian and Muslim. In short, where in all of human history is there one human who stands justified, perfect in love for God and neighbour?

Temptation 4: False Despair

If the eighteenth century gave impetus to the magical temptation of false hope, then surely the twentieth century assaulted humanity with the temptation of false despair. It was then that humankind applied its mastery of philosophy and science to unleash a hundred years of war and mass murder that slaughtered an estimated 170–213 million people.

In the aftermath, conditions did not favour the temptation to hope in human perfectibility, but were ideal for its mirror image – the futility of any hope at all. Existential despair became the final stop on the line.

But this is just more of the same. Both false hope and false despair hold the same mistaken assumption about humans, namely, that mankind is the key to mankind's great quest for life. It naturally follows that, if mankind has no hope in itself, then mankind must have no hope at all. Those who believe that humans are doomed are as mistaken as those who think that the success of human goodness is just ahead.

For the person who seeks God, the temptation of false despair tries to obscure every possibility that God is present and active in his creation. But religious scriptures present a completely different picture.

Whatever holy book you choose, you must note its ardent hope for humans. The nontheistic scriptures ultimately locate those hopes within the self; the monotheistic scriptures locate them in the Almighty; and each of the monotheistic scriptures hopes in the Almighty in different ways and for different reasons. All this you will have to ponder and come to understand. But in any scripture, you will find that hopelessness is not the final story.

Consider the Christian scripture in particular. Perhaps in no other book and in no other religion is there so extravagant a vision of hope for humans, for the whole of creation and for the future. In brief, the hope starts in Genesis when God reclaims Adam and Eve after their betrayal and tells them he will be with them even in their exile. In time, God expands his promise when he comes unbidden to Abram and promises him, for no reason other than God's generosity, that Abram's descendents will be God's means of blessing all of mankind. The entire story of Israel becomes the story of this ultimate destiny of blessing, however wayward and winding Israel's path through history may be. In the Christian scripture, the story of God's blessing to all through Israel leads to the story of God's redemption of every person through the messiah, God's new liberator of his chosen people. But now the chosen are all peoples and the liberation is from their oldest, deepest enslavement to sin and death. Moreover, the all-powerful love of God's messiah, Jesus of Nazareth, also liberates the entire creation. In Revelation, the final book of the New Testament, John says that he sees 'a new heaven and a new earth' (21:1). This is the ultimate goal of God's work, begun so long ago and far away in Eden. Mankind does not just return to the first Eden, but is part of a renewed, perfect creation where all things, all creatures, all people everywhere, in all time and space, live in completed love and the inexpressible ecstasy of God's presence.

This is why the apostle Paul spoke of the hope bestowed by Christ as wonderful beyond conceiving, literally unimaginable in its blessedness. George MacDonald, the great Scottish Victorian novelist and mystic, said, 'it is impossible for a man to see God as He is and not desire Him'. In the new heaven and the new earth, everyone sees God as he is – and every desire is filled to overflowing.

Temptation Unmasked

A firm stand against all these magical temptations – false unity, false separation, false hope, false despair – is essential in the search for God, but ultimately a true search requires a sober and mature self-search. It requires an unflinching encounter with oneself that goes deeper than politics, economics and culture. It may come quickly or slowly, in swift radiance or in great struggle. But come it must. In *The Gulag Archipelago*, Alexander Solzhenitsyn recounts the suffering and death of millions in the Soviet slave labour camp system. He also tells of his own imprisonment there and of his unexpected encounter with himself. He writes famously that 'It gradually became clear to me that the line dividing good and evil does not run between states, classes or parties. It runs through every human heart… It is impossible to drive evil out of the world altogether, but it is possible to try to drive it out of every individual.'[13]

Each of us has crossed the line, reaching for the forbidden fruit and the false promise that we can be like God. This fundamental, magical temptation is always before us in a thousand disguises. Even our best intentions can be subverted by our secret attraction to self-aggrandizement. As for our secret attraction, we can be the last ones to know about it.

That is why a true encounter with God requires, even beyond open-mindedness, a deep open-heartedness. Each person must face himself and his ancient temptation to be God. He must turn away from the false power of magic. He must turn to God and present himself just as he is.

Start Searching, Keep Searching

At this point, perhaps you find yourself with fewer illusions and greater humility about God. If so, you are richly equipped to start or renew your quest for the Source, the Centre, the Almighty, the Lord. You are free to begin right now. And take heart as you do, for God has long since launched his own great historic quest to find everyone who seeks. Including you.

Notes

1. All numbers for each religion's worldwide adherents are found at http://www.adherents.com/Religions_By_Adherents.html. Of its numbers, www.adherents.com says this: 'A major source for these estimates is the detailed country-by-country analysis done by David B. Barrett's religious statistics organization, whose data are published in the *Encyclopedia Britannica* (including annual updates and yearbooks) and also in the *World Christian Encyclopedia* (the latest edition of which – published in 2001 – has been consulted). Hundreds of additional sources providing more thorough and detailed research about individual religious groups have also been consulted.' Accessed 3 Jan 2008.

2. 'Among Wealthy Nations… U.S. Stands Alone in its Embrace of Religion', 19 Dec 2002, *The Pew Research Center for the People and the Press*. http://people-press.org/reports/. Accessed 13 Aug 2007.

3. Baggini, Julian, *Atheism: A Very Short Introduction* (Oxford: Oxford University Press, 2003), 98.

4. Webb, Jeffrey, *The Complete Idiot's Guide To Exploring God* (New York: Alpha Books, 2005), 273–75.

5. 'Major Religions of the World Ranked by Number of Adherents', *Adherents.com*. http://www.adherents.com/Religions_By_Adherents.html#Neo-Paganism. Accessed 13 Aug 2007.

6. Spong, John Shelby, 'A Call for a New Reformation', *The Diocese of Newark Online*. http://www.dioceseofnewark.org/jsspong/reform.html.

7. Ibid.

8. Ibid.

9. Spong, John Shelby, *Why Christianity Must Change Or Die: A Bishop Speaks To Believers In Exile* (San Francisco: HarperSanFrancisco, 1998), 55.

10. 'Very few countries have witnessed a dramatic rise in Christianity as it occurred in Korea within a few decades of the twentieth century. According to the CIA factbook, the Christians and Buddhists are each 26% of the population. Other sources claim the Christians are about 49%. The discrepancy arises because a large proportion of the population does not officially adhere to an organized religion. In any case, Christianity has overtaken Buddhism in Korea in four decades during 1960s–1980s "Conversion Boom" period.' From 'Christianity in Korea', *Wikipedia*. http://en.wikipedia.org/wiki/Christianity_in_Korea. Accessed 4 Jan 2008.

11. Elegant, Simon, 'The War for China's Soul', 20 Aug 2006, *Time Magazine*. http://www.time.com/time/magazine/article/0,9171,1229123,00.html. Accessed 31 Oct 2007.

12. Pickthall, M. M., *The Meaning of the Glorious Qur'an* (Beltsville, Maryland: Amana Publications, 1999), 636.

13. Quoted in 'Islands of Slavery', 24 June 1974, *Time Magazine*. http://www.time.com/time/magazine/article/0,9171,944884,00.html. Accessed 10 Dec 2007.

Bibliography

Armstrong, Karen, *History of God*. New York: Gramercy Books, 1993.

Baggini, Julian, *Atheism: A Very Short Introduction*. Oxford: Oxford University Press, 2003.

Barker, Dan, *Losing Faith In Faith: From Preacher to Atheist*. Madison, WI: Freedom From Religion Foundation, Inc., 2006.

Barrett, David B. et al., *World Christian Encyclopedia, Second Edition*. New York: Oxford University Press, 2001.

Campbell, Jeremy, *The Many Faces of God: Science's 400-Year Quest For Images of the Divine*. New York: W. W. Norton & Co., 2006.

Cook, Michael, *The Koran: A Very Short Introduction*. New York: Oxford University Press, 2000.

Esack, Farid, *The Qur'an: A User's Guide*. Oxford: Oneworld Publications, 2005.

Harbour, Daniel, *An Intelligent Person's Guide to Atheism*. London: Gerald Duckworth Ltd., 2001.

Keener, Craig S., *The IVP Bible Background Commentary, New Testament*. Downers Grove, IL: InterVarsity Press, 1993.

Lovegrove, J. W., *What is Islam?* The Mosque, Woking: Trust for the Encouragement and Circulation of Muslim Religious Literature, 1926.

McGrath, Alister, *The Twilight of Atheism: The Rise and Fall of Disbelief in the Modern World*. New York: Doubleday, 2004.

McGrath, Alister, *Dawkins' God: Genes, Memes, and the Meaning of Life*. Boston: Blackwell Publishing, 2006.

Metzger and Coogan, eds., *The Oxford Guide to Ideas & Issues of the Bible*. Oxford: Oxford University Press, 2001.

Nasir, S. H., *The Heart of Islam*. New York: HarperCollins Publishers, 2002.

Pickthall, M. M., *The Meaning of the Glorious Qur'an*. Beltsville, MD: Amana Publications, 1999.

Ryken, Wilhout, Longman et al., eds., *Dictionary of Biblical Imagery*. Downers Grove, IL: InterVarsity Press, 1998.

Sarwar, Muhammad and Toropov, Brandon, *The Complete Idiot's Guide to the Koran*. New York: Alpha Books, 2004.

Smart and Hecht, eds., *Sacred Texts of the World: A Universal Anthology*. New York: Crossroad Publishing Co., 1982.

Walton, Matthews and Chavalas, *The IVP Bible Background Commentary, Old Testament*. Downers Grove, IL: InterVarsity Press, 2000.

Webb, Jeffrey, *The Complete Idiot's Guide to Exploring God*. New York: Alpha Books, 2005.

Index